"My life was influenced as a teenager when I heard the testimony of Bro. D.C. Kaushal in All India Pentecostal Convention in Chandigarh. What follows is his adventurous journey with Jesus Christ and body of believers, full of excitement and challenges, the Cross, and the joy of the Lord. His story will encourage those who are changed by Christ to take up their cross and follow Him."

Rev. Dr. Richard Howell, Secretary EFICC
Principal, Caleb Institute of Theology
General Secretary, Asia Evangelical Alliance

"The story of my dear brother D.C. Kaushal's life is indeed a story worth telling. It is a story of faith, courage, conviction and clarity. His life is one worth imitating and imparting to many generations. If the book of Acts continues to be written in the lives of all of those who seek to honor our Lord and move and minister by his Spirit, then this book testifies to that dynamic reality.

"I have always known this was a chosen servant and and anointed apostolic leader of the highest order. His life has been marked by servanthood and selflessness in sharing the good news of Jesus Christ's love and power with everyone, everywhere. He has known suffering and success and trial and triumph. His devotion to Jesus is deep. His ministry for Jesus is dynamic. Yes, this is a story worth telling and a life worthy of faithful imitation and emulation. This book will instruct, impart, and inspire all who read it."

Dale Evrist
Founding/Senior Pastor
New Song Christian Fellowship, Nashville

"In the world, there are some rare people who leave their mark behind. They don't need to elaborate about themselves. They make their marks as they move forward. Bro. D.C. Kaushal is one of those rare people. Bro. Kaushal has led a life full of challenges, before as well as after coming to Christ. But amidst all this, one thing that kept him going was Christ's faithfulness."

Rev. V. S. Bhandari
Founder/Director, Agape, Dehradun (U.K) India

"I thank Lord Jesus Christ for the life of Bro. D.C. Kaushal. When the Lord moved in His servant's life, then his life became a blessing for many people. Because it is the promise of God that whosoever believes and obeys Him, He shall make him a source of blessing for all the nations of the earth."
Pastor Dr. Laji Paul
Vice President, IPC, Training & Development
Chairman, Living Hope Ministries

"I had the privilege to meet Bro. Kaushal in Punjab, when he was leading Every Home Crusade in the northwest with an army of young men. I saw a father and an army general in him. I see him as my elder brother and mentor. I am glad that he penned his life story at this time before he is promoted to glory."
Dr. P.G. Varghese
Founder, Indian Evangelical Team, www.pgv.com

"I have waited a long time for this story to be told. Over the years, I have heard bits and pieces, but this is my first time hearing all of it. Bro. D.C. is one of the finest, dedicated men I know. His life is a living example of hope for all who are looking for the evidence of God's redemption and purpose in each of us. I encourage you to read this book and be challenged in your own life to do greater things in the kingdom of God."
Dr. James Graham
President, International Gospel Outreach

"I came to India the first time in 1996 to find a ministry we could work with in reaching the people of India. We went away thinking that Living Hope was involved in the type of ministry we were looking for. D.C. Kaushal is an apostolic man and church planter, who was training men for church planting and who had high integrity. I have returned eleven times and was encouraged by the work of the Living Hope pastors and their leadership team."
Pastor Jim Shaw
Manukau New Life Church, New Zealand

FROM ROADSIDE TO THE ROYAL FAMILY

D.C. KAUSHAL

Newburg, Pennsylvania

From Roadside to the Royal Family—My Life Story
by D.C. Kaushal
Copyright ©2018 by Living Hope Ministries

All rights reserved. No part of this publication may be reproduced in any form or by any means, electronic or mechanical, including photocopying, recording, or any information storage and retrieval system, without written permission from the publisher.

Scripture is taken from the Holy Bible, New Living Translation, copyright ©1996. Used by permission of Tyndale House Publishers, Inc., Wheaton IL.

Printed in India.

ISBN 978-0-9860923-9-8

LIVING HOPE MINISTRIES
B-101, Palam Apartments,
Najafgarh Road, Bijwasan, New Delhi - 110061
M +91-92052-58018 • E-Mail: lhm@vsnl.com

Relate2God Press
PO Box 428
Newburg, PA 17240

Table of Contents

Chapter 1 – Family Background *1*
    Father's Untimely Death *1*
    Oppression at Home *2*

Chapter 2 – In Search of Truth *4*
    Experience of Salvation *6*
    Meeting with a Christian Tailor *6*
    The Christian Nurse *7*
    Steps towards Salvation *8*

Chapter 3 – Beginning of Christian Life *11*
    Testimony and Persecution *11*
    Thrown out of the House *12*
    Beginning of Christian Teachings and Baptism *12*
    The Key of Blessings *13*

Chapter 4 – Beginning of Ministry *15*
    Serving in S.P.C.K. Publishers *16*
    Bible Society of India, New Delhi *16*
    Redman Sisters *18*

Chapter 5 – God the Provider *20*
    Marriage *20*
    Pain, Hurt and Humiliation *24*
    Moving to the Bible Seminary *26*
    Ministry among the Korku Tribe *26*

Chapter 6 – Serving with Every Home Crusade *29*
    Workers for Harvest *30*
    Deliverance *32*
    An Unforgettable Incident *39*
    Himmat Lal and the Village Chief *40*
    Brother Guman Chand *41*
    Living Testimony - Kaleb Kerketta *42*
    Sukhram – S.R. Samuel *45*
    Struggle of Dhaniram *49*

Chapter 7 – Door to Door Visiting Jammu and Kashmir *53*
    Jehovah Jireh *53*
    Attention Gone; Accident On! *55*

    The Difficult Journey to Leh-Ladakh   *57*
    Sharing the Gospel in Leh-Ladakh   *58*
    Opposition from Muslim Fundamentalists   *59*
    Christ-Group Formation   *61*
    A Bitter Root – Anger   *62*
    New Vision   *66*

Chapter 8 – Miracle in New York   *69*

Chapter 9 – Formation of Living Hope Ministries   *74*

Chapter 10 – Ministry Expansion   *76*
    Badluram's Life Changed!   *76*
    Transformation of Ashok Kumar   *79*
    Growth of the Church   *80*
    Dayasagar Film   *80*

Chapter 11 – Adult Literacy Programme   *86*
    A Testimony of Mrs. Chinder   *87*
    My Life Changed by Dharampal   *89*
    And the Child Came Back to Life   *91*

Chapter 12 – Cried Seeing The Poverty   *94*
    Children's Home at Dharamgarh Odisha   *94*
    God Who Meets Our Needs   *95*
    Meeting Dave Bullock   *96*
    Some of Those Miracles   *98*
    Meeting God's Servant   *102*
    Meeting Bill Barr and his Mother   *105*
    Bible School Shifted to Gurgaon   *106*
    The Road Accident   *107*

Chapter 13 – Mercy Children's Home, Amritsar   *111*
    Aanchal   *113*

Chapter 14 – Pastor's Serving LHM   *115*
    Living Hope School—Gurugram   *117*
    Miracle after Miracle in Gurugram   *118*
    Firstborn Belongs to the Lord   *120*
    Basant Lama   *126*

Acknowledgments

With a grateful heart I give thanks to God, our Father and our Lord and Saviour Jesus Christ, who not only saved me, but enabled me to serve Him in the fullness of His Holy Spirit. I thank my wife, Sona, who has been with me in all the aspects of my life and supported me in writing this life story. I am also thankful to those friends, who helped me in translating this book from Hindi version into English.

And to those who contributed in editing: Mrs. Cheryl J. Barr, Pastor Keith Carroll, and Dr. Rev. Richard Howell.

To my wife, Sona,
our children and grandchildren,
all God's servants, and our friends
who have contributed to each area of ministry,
encouraged and sustained me by prayers.

Introduction

My purpose for writing this book is that I have learned to walk trusting in the faithfulness of God by faith. My Pastor M.K. Chacko taught me to walk by faith based on the Word of God. The key phrase on the subject that he shared was in Genesis 12. When God called Abram, it is written in verse 4, "And Abram started walking trusting God..."

I have experienced and seen that when I received the Lord's vision and started walking by faith, the Lord did not leave me. I have experienced God's faithfulness in each and every circumstances. The only true God, neither did He leave me nor did He deceive me. "To Him be the glory!" (Josua 1:5b)

I give all credit to my Lord Jesus Christ in writing of this book and believe that His name be honoured and glorified through this book. It is His grace on me that I could share the experiences of my life through this book. It is my earnest prayer, while many people will read this book, they will know the goodness of God. He is great, loving, compassionate, and merciful. He is faithful and He is faithful according to His Word.

God's faithfulness is the foundation of my life and the purpose of writing this book. May this book be a source of blessings to your life. Amen!

D.C. KAUSHAL
LIVING HOPE MINISTRIES

1

Family Background

You made all the delicate, inner parts of my body and knit me together in my mother's womb. Thank you for making me so wonderfully complex! Your workmanship is marvelous—how well I know it (Psalm 139:13-14).

Father's Untimely Death

I was only eight years old that fateful November day in 1944. We were a farming family in the Rohtak district of Punjab province, which is now part of Haryana. My father had five more brothers, and we had about three hundred bigha of land (about 75 acres).

My father was administering medicine to one of our sick buffalos when it abruptly struck my father's chest. He fell to the ground and was rushed to a government hospital in Bahadurgarh. After a few days, he expired. Other than this heart wrenching incident, I don't remember much about my father.

My father had been the head of the family. After his death, the overall responsibility of the house came upon his younger brother. Mother was now a widow. My brother, two sisters, and I became as helpless orphans. It was unbearable and difficult for me to accept my father's death. I often cried and stayed quiet. I missed him intensely.

Oppression at Home

I was often sent to the nearby pond to water the animals. One day while I took the buffaloes near the water to drink, our buffalo started to fight with another man's buffalo. Wrestling and tangling their curly horns with each other, they reached the middle of the pond where the water was deep. Both struggled and lost control. Helplessly, I stood by and witnessed our buffalo drown to death in the water.

With great difficulty, we somehow tied our buffalo with ropes and pulled it out of the pond. Total blame for our buffalo's death was put on me. After this, my uncle beat me for every little mistake. Day after day I fell prey to the wrath of my third uncle, sometimes without any mistake and sometimes due to the mistakes of others.

Utterly broken, I got lost in my thoughts and cried in loneliness. In this joint family, only my mother was compassionate towards me and comforted me. No one put a loving hand upon my head. I had no one with whom I could share my pain because my mother was too busy with household chores. Memories remain to this day of those oppressions that I suffered at their hands during my tender years. My elder brother and my two sisters also suffered the same wrath and torture. One day I was asked to take lunch to the fields for my youngest uncle and elder brother. When I reached there, they were plugging the field. I put the lunch under a sheet next to my uncle's and brother's sheets. The moment my uncle saw the lunch covered with that sheet, he became very furious and he beat me mercilessly with a rod.

I did not know that the sheet belonged to our labourer, who

Family Background

was not of our caste. I returned home crying. I just could not understand why this was happening to me.

I failed the eighth class so was beaten again. Because of these brutalities, hatred and loneliness, one day I ran away from home to find peace. Instead, I found only disappointment. After a few days, I returned home. More thrashings welcomed me home. Scars of my childhood remain on many parts of my body, reminding me of my troubled childhood.

2

In Search of Truth

Then he takes what's left and makes his god: a carved idol! He falls down in front of it, worshiping and praying to it. "Recuse me!" he says. "You are my god!" Such stupidity and ignorance! Their eyes are closed, and they cannot see. Their minds are shut, and they cannot think" (Isaiah 44:17-18).

In 1953, construction work on our new house began and progressed rapidly. This house was large because my father was one of six brothers. All families lived and worked in the field together and shared a common kitchen. The new house had thirteen rooms including sitting area for each family and separate guest rooms. Specially ordered stones from Rajasthan were fixed at the most important places of the house.

By the entrance of our house was a courtyard. Between the two doors was a way to go into the adjacent three rooms with a window-like space in between. Nobody knew about this space. All the laborers left for their home except for the stone craftsman. His work was to be completed in another one or two days. He told

In Search of Truth

my uncle that it was considered auspicious to place a statue of the home god Hanuman towards the north side since it was the best location. Then my uncle told him to look for a suitable stone for the idol. He saw a broken and useless stone, which was used by men of the family for bathing. The stone craftsman lifted the stone, wiped and cleaned it with a cloth, and let it dry. Then, using chalk, he drew a figure of the family god, Hanuman on it. I watched all this in great amazement. When he was about to carve the statue of Hanuman with hammer and chisel, I became impatient. I gathered all my courage to confront the craftsman, who was about eleven feet away from me. "Mistri Ji, how can you carve the god's image on this stone, how will it answer our prayers?" The moment he heard my question, he became angry. He threatened to complain about me to my third uncle. My uncle was legalistic in his opinions and everyone in the house feared him. I became afraid after hearing this and said no more. But uncontrollable restlessness agitated my heart.

Then the craftsman returned to work, finished, and placed the idol in the empty space. Within a week he installed the idol. Our family priest led the family to worship the idol. The rest of the family joined him in worship with full fervor. Unwillingly I also joined them, keeping all these questions in my heart. The more I looked at the idol, the more my heart yearned to know the truth.

After the craftsman finished all his work, affectionately he instructed me, "Wake up every day at 5 o'clock in the morning, bathe, read the Hanuman Paath and meditate daily. If you follow this, you will surely have peace in your heart."

Upon his saying this, I made it my life style. I relentlessly meditated on it for seven years. Even after such rigorous meditation, I never felt peace or experienced deliverance. Instead, my hunger for truth intensified, and I performed my rituals with more seriousness. With full responsibility and earnestness, I fulfilled all the requirements such as fasting in order to perform the rituals. Despite all this, I felt a vacuum in my heart. I was restless and felt something was missing in my life.

Experience of Salvation

Even before he made the world, God loved us and chose us in Christ to be holy and without fault in his eyes. God decided in advance to adopt us into his own family by bringing us to himself through Jesus Christ. This is what he wanted to do, and it gave him great pleasure (Ephesians 1:4-5).

In December 1959, I was studying in Ahir College, Rewari Punjab (Haryana State since November 1966) and lived in the college hostel. During the winter, I suddenly caught a very high fever. Seeing me suffering from high fever, the hostel warden Professor Balbir Singh Yadav sent me with the watchman to see a doctor. I was diagnosed with pneumonia. The doctor advised me to take one chicken egg along with lukewarm milk every morning for a speedy recovery.

Meeting with a Christian Tailor

The doctor's advice of eating an egg daily shook me. Strongly grounded in Hinduism, our family was very proud of our orthodox (Sanatan Dharma) religion. If I ate eggs, it could corrupt my religion. So, I decided that, no matter what comes, I would not eat eggs. When the doctor saw no improvement in my condition, he forced me to drink milk and take eggs with the assertion that I must take these as a daily dose. On my way to the college hostel, I encountered a tailor whose house was on the same street where I walked daily to and from college. Many chickens roamed around his house. He was a Christian.

One day the tailor gave me a book by Sadhu Sundar Singh, which was titled *With and Without Christ*. It was in the Urdu language. Returning to the hostel, I started to read this book. Every word of this book pierced my heart. I felt like it was revealing everything about my miserable life. *What a wretched man I am!* I recognised that I was living a deeply sinful life and moving towards hell. I realised that, if I repented and confessed my sins, believed in the Lord Jesus Christ, and accepted Him as my Lord and Saviour, I could experience salvation in my life. Doing this, I would live in His presence now and for eternity. All this would happen because Jesus bore my sins on the cross and shed His blood to pay a complete price for my salvation. He passed through death, rose from the dead on the third day with a living hope and is alive today. It was 17 January, 1960.

The Christian Nurse

I wanted to know more. But sometimes I doubted, wondering if these concepts were illusions. Getting to the root of this truth became my purpose. Many questions arose in my thoughts. I met with some people in this context but could not come to any conclusion.

The examination of our college was cancelled because the question paper was out; therefore, all the students were sent to different colleges for re-examination in the state. I was sent to a Dharmashala in Kangra district. Some students had gone along with me. But one day, while I was returning to my room after finishing my exam, I met a nurse who was waiting for a bus at a nearby bus stop facing the hospital. Sensing that she might be a Christian, I stopped and asked,

"Sister, are you a Christian?"

She answered in bewilderment, "Yes, I am! But why are you asking?"

"I want to know about Lord Jesus Christ," I said. "Do you know any person who can tell me everything about Jesus?" After listening, she was very pleased, gave me an address, and said, "There is a prayer meeting in the evening at this place, please do come. You will get the answers to all your questions."

Steps Towards Salvation

It was a Thursday. I reached the address in the evening the nurse had given me. There the Gospel preachers O.J. Wilson and M.K. Chacko were preaching from the Bible. I saw a crowd standing across the street, listening to the preaching. I also joined them to listen. While listening to the message, I felt like they were speaking about my life.

My exams were over and I had plenty of time, so the next day I again went there. During the preaching I again felt like they were preaching about my life. That day after the meeting, I went to the preacher O.J. Wilson and asked, "How do you know about me?"

"I don't understand!" he said.

"I am asking because what you were preaching was all about my life," I said.

He laughed. "Brother, I don't even know you! Who are you?" Then I told him briefly about my life and said, "I am in search of true peace." He explained salvation and inner peace through Jesus Christ and said, "If you believe in the Lord Jesus Christ, then assuredly you will have peace and salvation." Indeed, I was in search of this. Both the preachers had stood by the roadside and preached in the evenings. It was Sunday the 8th of May 1960, the last day of the public meeting. The next morning, I returned to the roadside spot early, but everything seemed deserted. I stood there disappointed. Then I heard Christian songs coming from a house nearby. Following the music. I easily found the house and knocked at the door.

Preacher O.J. Wilson opened the door and, upon seeing me, asked, "Brother, have you found peace?" With full honesty, I replied, "No, sir!"

"There is no magic in my hands to lay upon you and give you peace," he said.

"Then what shall I do to get peace?" I asked.

He called me inside, opened his Bible, and explained in detail about salvation through the Lord Jesus Christ. He said, "Open your heart and cast all your burdens on the Lord Jesus and pray to the Lord Jesus in the way two best friends talk to each other." Further he said, "Surely, if you do this, you will have peace. Your sins will be forgiven, and you will receive new life. Come on your knees and open your heart to God, and you will surely see a miracle."

At that time, including the two preachers, there were only eight people in that room. This house was Dr. Ms. Marian's house from Andhra Pradesh, and she had her clinic on the ground floor. As he said, I knelt on the floor and starting confessing all my sins. While I was confessing my sins, I felt a wonderful touch on my left shoulder. I sat down and saw as I opened my eyes, a bright, shining light rising like sunlight and spreading across the room from one corner of the ceiling. I realised God's presence, and His fear captured my heart. I wept vigorously, confessing my sins and continued asking forgiveness from the Lord Jesus. It was a marvelous experience. All the painful burdens left my heart. A cold gust of wind had passed over me, and after that, I experienced great peace which surpasses all understanding. My heart was filled with joy. Praise the Lord!

As I opened my eyes after some time, Preacher Wilson asked, "What happened to you?" I could not explain this experience in words. It was as if he had asked a mute man how a chocolate tasted. He can only communicate by signs. The happiness, peace, and joy I received cannot be acquired anywhere in this world. God's love is beyond comprehension. To Him be the glory!

> *So now there is no condemnation for those who belong to Christ Jesus. And because you belong to him, the power of the life-giving Spirit has freed you from the power of sin that leads to death* (Romans 8:1-2).

> *Therefore, since we have been made right in God's sight by faith, we have peace with God because of what Jesus Christ our Lord has done for us* (Romans 5:1).

The next day I returned to my village.

3

Beginning of Christian Life

In his kindness God called you to share in his eternal glory by means of Christ Jesus. So after you have suffered a little while, he will restore, support, and strengthen you, and he will place you on a firm foundation (1 Peter 5:10).

After this amazing experience with the Lord, I headed towards home with great anticipation. I wanted to reach home as soon as possible to tell about this good news of my salvation. Because I felt amazing joy and peace, I thought that my family members should also know and gladly accept this.

Testimony and Persecution

After reaching home, first I confronted my third uncle. I told him about my experience and said, "I have accepted the Lord Jesus Christ as my Lord and Saviour." Upon hearing this, he became furious and beat me brutally with a rod, gathered everyone around, and shouted that I had become an apostate to the whole family.

My uncle was of an orthodox belief. He looked at Christians with hatred, and this decision was unbearable for him. His behaviour toward me turned into full hatred. But thanks to the Lord Jesus Christ who did not let the seed of bitterness flourish in my heart. I praise my great and wonderful

Lord Jesus Christ because He is loving, exceedingly merciful and compassionate. He loves the sinner.

Thrown Out of the House

The event took place a year after my engagement. As soon as news of my faith in Jesus Christ was known by my future would be in-laws, they immediately called off the engagement. When my family heard that, again they were furious and began to curse me. They got very angry at me and said, "You have ruined the family's name by becoming a Christian." So far, I did not even know that I was a Christian. I had simply accepted the Lord Jesus Christ as my personal Saviour, had remission of sins, and was saved from all the curses through faith in Jesus Christ.

I have not forgotten that June night in 1960. To save the family from defamation, my family brutally beat me half dead and threw me out of the house. With much pain and anguish, I struggled to walk five miles towards the Bahadurgarh railway station. I had no money, no clothes, nor did I know where I should go. I had the address of Ps. M.K. Chacko, this was given to me by Ps. O.J. Wilson, saying if I ever went to Delhi, I needed to meet Ps. Chacko. I thought maybe he might help me.

Beginning of Christian Teachings and Baptism

The next morning, 5th June 1960 I took a train to Delhi without a ticket, arriving in Sarai Rohilla, Delhi. I headed straight towards Karol Bagh, Christian Colony to Ps. M.K. Chacko's house. When I reached it, I knocked at his door. First, he looked at me carefully because I was in an unrecognisable condition. Then, when he realised who I was, he lovingly hugged me and took me in. I explained the recent turn of events. He consoled me and said, "Don't worry my brother; God must have a plan in this." Then he prayed for me and arranged for my stay. I lived in his home for two months. I am indebted to him for a lifetime for such a favor.

The Key of Blessings

It was a Sunday, and the worship meeting started at 9 am sharp. The worshippers glorified the Lord with songs of praise. After that, it was time for testimonies. Many people testified about the work the Lord did in their lives. Then Pastor Chacko asked me, "Bro. Kaushal, you also share your testimony." I stood up and started telling about my marvellous experience at Dharmashala of Kangra district. I tried to describe that experience, but it was very difficult to explain. I sounded like a mute man trying to describe how the chocolate tasted that he had just eaten.

After the service, everyone left for their homes except for Ps. Chacko, an elderly sister, and me. That woman called me to her and handed me something like an offering. Quietly, without looking to see what it was, I put it in my pocket. Ps. Chacko was watching. After the woman left, the pastor asked, "Did that sister gave you something?"

"Yes!" I replied. "What did she give you?" he asked.

I reached into my pocket and showed the pastor what that sister had given to me. It was a two rupee note.

Then the pastor asked, "Can you see that box on the table in front of you?"

"Yes," I replied.

"Put a tenth of that offering in the box," he said.

I replied, "But I don't have any change to put in the offering box."

"Do one thing, go to Prahlad Market and get the change." I immediately went to Prahlad Market, which was nearby, and got the change.

Then the pastor said, "Come, let us first give thanks for this offering."

I didn't know how to give thanks and ask for the blessings upon the offering.

"Keep this money in your hand," he said. Then he laid his hands upon my hands and gave thanks to the Lord on my behalf. He instructed me to put a tenth of two rupees, which was twenty paisa, into the offering box. "From today onwards, never forget to give a tenth to the Lord," he said. "If you will do this, then surely God will bless you, and you will never lack anything in life."

That day I truly learned to give my tenth to the Lord, and through that tenth (20 Paisa) offering, God has blessed my life and my family in countless ways. Hallelujah!

Today, who I am and what I have is by the grace of our Lord Jesus Christ. I learnt that, when we cheerfully and gladly give, the Lord blesses our lives abundantly. Then in obedience to our Lord, on Sunday June 6, 1960, I was immersed in water baptism by Pastor Chacko in the Yamuna River by the I.S.B.T. Kashmiri Gate bus terminal. Bro. Kailash Rana, Bro. A.B. Teju and other believers from church were present at the time of the baptism. During my stay at Ps. M.K. Chacko's home, he taught me many lessons from the Bible. Pastor C.V. Robert taught me how to pray.

All the believers devoted themselves to the apostles' teaching, and to fellowship, and to sharing in meals (including the Lord's Supper), and to prayer. (Acts 2:42).

Praise the Lord Jesus!

4

Beginning of Ministry

That is what the Scriptures mean when they say,

No eye has seen, no ear has heard, and no mind has imagined what God has prepared for those who love him (1 Corinthians 2:9).

After being baptised, I went to Hardoi, Uttar Pradesh, to study the Bible from 1960 until 1963. Since I had no prior biblical knowledge, these studies were very difficult. Miss Ann R. Eberheart, principal of the Bible school, was a missionary serving with the Assemblies of God Missions. She helped me in every possible way with studies and other daily needs. After completing my Bible course in March 1963, I was about to return to Delhi when she asked, "Do you want to study further?"

"It will be in English?" I asked despairingly. I did not understand English much, and my English grammar was very poor.

"I will bear the entire cost of your fees," she replied. "Also, I would happily pay the tuition cost for three months for you to learn the English language and grammar."

I asked for a little time to think and pray for God's leading. After two days I answered her with a yes and went to Bangalore for further Bible studies. There I met three more brothers, who were weak in English. We completed a three-month English course taught by T.P. James. In March 1964, I completed the English Bible course. I was amazed how God blessed me through so many different people. Our God is a loving and caring God.

Serving in S.P.C.K. Publishers

God slowly prepared me for His service. After returning from Bangalore, I worked in one of the branches of S.P.C.K. Publishing London in Delhi from April 1964 to July 1965 as a salesman. This bookshop was in Kashmiri Gate, Delhi. Along with working here, I regularly participated in services at Karol Bagh Church. Through prayers, testimonies, God's Word, and fellowship, I grew in the Christian faith. Also, I regularly gave the Lord's portion joyfully as my pastor had taught me on the very first day.

I became uncomfortable working in the S.P.C.K. bookshop. Most of the workers were worldly, using abusive language. The executive secretary, who lived above the bookshop, drank almost every day after lunch. Returning to work afterwards, he argued and abused the first person to confront him. I always kept my distance from these things. I sought advice from others, including Bro. George Nyberg in whose house I lived as a paying guest. He was like my elder brother in faith. He spent time in prayer and in the Word with me as did Bro. Kailash Rana. I shared my problem with my pastor and asked what I should do.

Bible Society of India, New Delhi

After much discussion with my pastor and Bro. Kailash Rana, I decided to serve with the Bible Society of India in Allahabad, U.P. so I sent my application to them. The Bible Society of India, New Delhi's secretary, Captain Sinclair, phoned me one day and asked, "Why do you want to go to Allahabad?" I was surprised that he knew about my application.

Beginning of Ministry

I said, "I want to serve."

"Come and meet me tomorrow at 9:00 a.m. at The Bible House, Parliament Street, New Delhi," he said.

The next day, July 31, 1965, I went to meet him. He asked me many questions and took down all the details about me. In short, I gave my testimony. He then prayed and said, "Start coming here tomorrow for work. No need to go to Allahabad."

I discussed this matter again with my pastor for advice. He prayed for me and said, "You can start working with the Bible Society of India, New Delhi tomorrow onward. It is a good opportunity."

From August 1, 1965 onwards, I served as an evangelist in the Bible Society. Then I was sent to Pastor Edward in Gwalior, MP to learn about Bible literature distribution. From there I went with Ps. G.M.S. Gill and Ps. Edward to many places with new experiences and came back to Delhi. At that time, the Operation Mobilization team distributed literature in the Old Delhi area. The Bible Society team also participated in this.

The Indo-Pak war was going on in those days, and many army personnel were admitted in wounded condition at various hospitals. Our team ministered to them, giving them a booklet about the Gospel of Matthew, titled *Sermon on the Mount*.

After ministering there for 40 days, the secretary of the Bible Society, Captain Sinclair, called me into his office. "Would you like to continue the work that you are doing past 40 days?" he asked.

"Yes sir!" I replied. Then he asked me to go for ministry in the state of Punjab. At that time, the Bible Society had a Willis Van of Mahindra Company that we used to take Bible literature for the hospitals, schools, streets markets, and fairs for distribution. Whenever we had the opportunity to go to churches for worship on Sundays, we introduced people to the Bible

Society's work. We distributed free literature in hospitals to all patients but charged a nominal price for the literature on the squares, streets, in markets, and at fairs. I served with the Bible Society in Haryana, Punjab, Himachal Pradesh, Chandigarh, Jammu and Kashmir, Leh-Ladakh and Rajasthan states and gave the Gospel to thousands. For such valuable opportunities to serve, I give thanks to the Lord Jesus!

In Kullu City, which is now merged in Himachal Pradesh, we went to the Dussehra fair, a major Hindu festival. This fair is held yearly in the month of October. With full preparations and prayers, we started our journey from Delhi. On the way, we stopped at many places like Karnal, Ambala, Khanna Mandi, Ludhiana, and Jalandhar. When we reached Pathankot, we ministered with Rev. D.K. Mall and the youth of his church on the streets, in schools, in hospitals, among the soldiers' army cantonment, and in Alvin Girls' School. Then from Pathankot, we traveled to Palampur.

Redman Sisters

Along with Ps. Yusuf Jagannath, we preached the Gospel in Palampur and distributed Bible literature at schools, market places, and to nearby village people. At that time, the two Redman sisters from England ministered in Palampur. I had the opportunity to serve with those sisters. We came to know about the local hilly areas and the local language of Kulluvi. While ministering with the Redman sisters, the Spirit of God taught me that we must be thankful to God in every matter.

Walking up the foothills towards the small villages to minister the Gospel, we stopped for lunch. The sisters saw a clean place and said, "Brother, let us eat something here." We sat down there, exhausted. One of the sisters took bread out from their bag, a bottle of tea, a bottle of jam, and a military personnel style water bag. I was surprised to see that they carried so many supplies because they were around 60 years old. One of the sisters opened a pack of bread that had mildew on it. But her face did not show any stress or anxiety. Instead she removed the mildew, spread the jam on it, and gave thanks to the Lord. Then they gave me a piece. Without hesitation, I took the bread, gave thanks to the Lord, and began to eat. Then she took bread, cleaned it, spread the jam, and gave it to Bro. John, our driver. But Bro. John refused to take the bread because he saw mildew on it. Those Redman sisters asked, "Brother, what happened? Why are you refusing to take it?"

"This bread had mildew on it," said Bro. John. "I don't want to get sick eating it."

Hearing this, both sisters started to cry. I couldn't understand what happened. Then the sisters said, "Bro. John, do you know that there are so many people in this world who do not have the privilege to eat even this food? But it is God's mercy that we have food to eat. Whatever we get, we should give thanks to God and eat it."

Despite this, Bro. John still refused to eat it. I know those sisters must have been hurt. The rest of us ate and gave thanks to the Lord. I was blessed to see the hard work and love of those sisters, and I learnt that we must give thanks to God in everything.

I remembered that my Pastor M.K. Chacko would say, "Shukar ho! Shukar ho! Thank You, Lord! Thank You, Lord!" for everything. As Paul also wrote,

> *Be thankful in all circumstances, for this is God's will for you who belong to Christ Jesus* (1 Thessalonians 5:18).

Later we went with those sisters to the Kullu fair to minister.

5

God the Provider

You bless the godly, O Lord; you surround them with your shield of love (Psalm 5:12).

"God will provide a sheep for the burnt offering, my son," Abraham answered. And they both walked on together (Genesis 22:8).

The Lord Jesus Christ did great favours in my life. When I remember them, my heart is filled with gratitude. He did more than I could ask or think of. May He be praised!

Marriage

One of the S.P.C.K. London bookshops was at Saint James Church Compound near Kashmiri Gate, Old Delhi. The bookshop was divided into three departments: the first was editorial, the second was a publication, and the third was the sales department. At that time, I worked in the sales department. In October 1964, I was sent to Meerut, UP to sell books at a conference for pastors from Anglican churches in various places. I set up the book exhibit. One day Pastor A.B. Samson of Bulandshahar, UP came to see the books.

After looking at the display, he asked me about my family. I gave him my testimony, telling him that my father and my mother had passed away. "After coming to Christian faith, my family threw me out of the house. Now I am alone."

"Brother, how many children do you have and what does your wife do?" he asked.

"Pastor Ji, I am single right now," I replied. "I am not yet married."

"Oh! Okay! So, you will get married soon?" he said.

"If the Lord provides, then of course I will," I said.

"What type of girl you want marry?" he asked. "Simple, educated, nurse, teacher?"

"Educated, and one who knows how to take care of house," I said. "If she is a trained teacher, then it would be better."

Smiling, he said, "You are very clever. Why not a nurse? She will bring more money and you can even go abroad."

"It is better to serve the Lord in one's own country," I replied.

After the conference ended, everyone returned to their places. I received a letter from Pastor Samson saying, "Come to our church and share your testimony at Bulandshahar, Uttar Pradesh."

I travelled 50 miles by bus to his church and gave my testimony the first Sunday of December, 1964. Afterwards, Pastor Ji took me to his home. Pastor Ji introduced me to his family while we waited to have the meal. A young woman was also sitting there.

Pastor Ji introduced me to her and said, "Bro. Kaushal, this is Sona. She is our school teacher." I perceived that the pastor was introducing us with the intent of marriage. Looking at me, he said, "You wanted to marry a teacher. Sona is a teacher. If you have any question, then please ask her."

We began to talk. I told Sona everything about myself. Then Pastor Ji asked Sona, "Do you like this young man? If you want to ask anything, then ask."

"What is your caste?" Sona asked.

"What kind of question is this?" I replied. "I am a Christian believer, and what does caste mean among Christians?"

"Due to some reasons, people still ask for caste for marriages," Pastor Ji explained. "Though coming to faith in Christ, many still follow their old traditions and values. Due to this, the woman going in marriage has to follow same traditions."

Now I understood his point. Pastor Ji prayed for me and I returned to Delhi. After some time, one morning when I was in the bookshop, a man wearing Dhoti-Kurta and a turban on his head, came in the bookshop and stood. Very humbly he asked me, "Does D.C. Kaushal work here?" "Yes sir, I am D.C. Kaushal."

Then he began to ask me questions. He took all the information about me, my family background, and my village. I was clueless why he asked such questions. I told him briefly how I came to know Jesus. Later I learned that he was none other than Sona's father, Jagram Singh. He took the information and arrived in my village, where he was welcomed very warmly. When he said that he was thinking about giving his daughter in marriage to D.C. Kaushal, my family members clearly said that they were no more related to me. "He has become a Christian and is dead for us now. He brought shame to our family."

After a few months, Pastor Samson again called me to his church in the second week of January 1965, and Sona was also there. After the church service he asked, "What have you decided?" I asked Sona about her spiritual experience. She said that she had accepted the Lord as her personal Lord and Saviour and was a member of the St. Paul Church.

I told Pastor Samson, "I have no objection for marriage. But first I will share with my pastor and church secretary. I will pray and take their advice. Then if the Lord leads me and them, I

God the Provider

will let you know my decision with their blessings. Please wait for the answer."

Upon asking Sona, she said, "I will do as my father says."

Pastor Ji said, "Your father is willing." Then he explained how her father went to my village. "Your family is satisfied with the information your father has gathered."

I did not like this and said, "Did he go to see elephants and horses there?" Pastor explained that every father in Christian families wants to be sure that his daughter is married to a true Christian family. He prayed and then I returned to Delhi.

Some more time passed and I began serving with the Bible Society from August 1965. I was in contact with Masihi Sahitya Sanstha (Christian Literature Institute) for work. Bro. Prempal Singh, Sona's elder brother, was working there.

D.C. & Sona Kaushal wedding

One day Bro. Prempal Singh asked me, "Bro. Kaushal, whatsoever the matter is, say it clearly. If it is yes for marriage, then it is fine; otherwise it is all right."

I replied, "My church secretary, Bro. Kailash Rana, and his wife would like to meet Sona and talk with her."

Then Bro. Prempal Singh called his sister Sona to Delhi. After meeting Sona, Mrs. and Bro. Kailash Rana were happy. Bro. Kailash Rana conveyed everything to Pastor M.K. Chacko and Bro. A.B. Teju, the church treasurer. They prayed and after fifteen days, with the blessings of our pastor and the church leaders, Sona and I were married on April 12, 1966 at Saint Paul Church, Bulandshahar, UP. God has blessed us with four children and seven grandchildren. God has blessed our family with manyfold blessings.

Let all that I am praise the Lord; with my whole heart, I will praise his holy name (Psalm 103:1).

Pain, Hurt and Humiliation

Since I had lost my father at a young age, I had no knowledge of how to maintain a family life. I depended upon my wife to care for the children and household matters. In the 1960s there was no teaching on family life in our church, but that is no excuse. I should have learned by observing our church families. Instead, I focused on the ministry.

On August 18, 1968, I started serving in Green Park, New Delhi, with Pastor M.K. Chacko, my Pastor Ji. He had gone to speak in a convention in Bihar State when two sisters from the USA came to speak at our Pentecostal church in late February of 1969. Both sisters rolled on the floor of the church after the message. These sisters wore short skirts, very inappropriate in Indian culture where women cover their legs. Our church women joined them, rolling on the floor. People from the neighborhood started coming to see what was happening. Ashamed, I tried to stop them but I couldn't.

India Every Home Crusade office was next to our church. The Director, Dr. P. N. Kurien, asked me to help them in a baptismal service of new believers in a village near Kanpur, U.P. about 400 Km from New Delhi Brother Maxton, the field coordinator, would go with me. One of our church member, Daya Ram, was working with IEHC as field evangelist, and he had given information about the baptism to Dr. Kurien. After walking about 21 kilometers to the village, we found out that no one had accepted Jesus as Lord and Savior so no one was ready for baptism. Disappointed, we left. On the way back to Delhi, Brother Maxton started commenting about Pentecostal believers. I was deeply ashamed of what he had observed.

The next Sunday, Pastor Ji went to another church convention in M.P. On his return, he told me that he had information about the sisters from the USA rolling on the floor. He asked if this really did happen. I said it was true. He had also heard that I had spoken about our Brother Daya Ram.

Without warning, Pastor Ji asked me to vacate the church room immediately. We were terribly shaken and did not know where to go. Our eldest son was barely two years old and our second was a newborn. The church split into two groups, one of which asked me to be their pastor. I refused with due respect as I never wanted to go against my Pastor Ji. I was very disappointed and humiliated because no church member spoke a word whether I was right or wrong. It took years for Sona to overcome the hurt.

A member of another church, who was private secretary to thebHonorable Prime Minister, helped us to get accommodations in Sarojini Nagar. Dr. Kurien offered for me to teach in his India Bible Institute near Safdarjung Enclave, far away from the church. I taught there for one year from April 1969 until March 1970. Then I went to Union Biblical Seminary, Yavatmal, Maharashtra with my family.

I was serving the Lord with IEHC Jaipur, Rajasthan, when I invited Pastor M.K.Chacko and Pastor Thomas Matthews to minister to our coworkers at meetings we held in the Udaipur auditorium. Pastor Ji stayed with me. On the third day, he called me to his room. Hugging me, he said, "You are my son and I am happy that the Lord is blessing you."

I felt accepted and loved by my pastor who had become as a father to me. Our relationship was restored. What a blessing. Praise the Lord!

Moving to the Bible Seminary

Give all your worries and cares to God, for he cares about you (1 Peter 5:7).

The Lord says, "I will guide you along the best pathway for your life. I will advise you and watch over you" (Psalm 32:8).

On August 18, 1968, I started serving the Lord with my Pastor M.K. Chacko in Green Park, New Delhi. While serving there, I felt the need for further studies and prayed earnestly about it. I spoke with Dr. I.Ban.Wati, General Secretary, of the Evangelical Fellowship of India about my interest in attending Union Biblical Seminary in Yavatmal, Maharashtra. He recommended me to the principal of UBS.

The Lord opened a door for me. In June 1970, I went to Union Bible Seminary with my wife, Sona, and our two sons, Subodh John and Sudhir Paul. The Lord provided accommodations and studies in a wonderful way. The Lord blessed our family through many people. Pastor Albert Adams, a friend of Dr. P.N. Kurien, met our family needs. Our monthly fee was paid by Doctor Humber Hattie, who was a retired judge of Bombay High Court from Ahmad Nagar, Maharashtra. Sona also completed a one year Bible course.

Ministry Among the Korku Tribe

In my desperation I prayed, and the Lord listened; he saved me from all my troubles (Psalm 34:6).

In October of 1971, our seminary's Evangelism Director Rev. Vern Middleton took a team of seven of us students for practical evangelistic work among the Korku people in the small town of Dharni, Amravati district. Rev. Vern Middleton's family lived in a Baptist mission bungalow.

God the Provider

As we were traveling on a muddy road through a deserted forest, the Jeep axle broke down about seven in the evening. It was silent everywhere with no village or mechanic in sight. Our only option was to walk 17 kilometres to Dharni and bring a mechanic back. It was almost dark.

"Who will go with me?" asked Rev. Middleton. Nobody answered. When he looked at me, I got ready. The two of us walked through the darkness, singing and praying. We feared the wild animals, but God protected us. Around 4 o'clock in the morning, we reached Dharni.

We returned the next day to our team who had sat around a campfire, praying through the night. The mechanic repaired our Jeep so we could finish our trip. During this visit to the Korku tribe, Rev. Middleton instructed that, before serving among any communities, we must pray. Then we must understand their language, lifestyle, behaviour, and worship methods. He said that it is always wise to contact the head of village or a tribal leader first. We needed to pray for the leader and tell him our purpose. And yes, if under the leading of the Holy Spirit, we should start sharing the Gospel. We were there for one week to learn.

The following year, Rev. Middleton asked us to spend the summer with them in the Chilkadara area of Amravati District. This area is mostly Korku tribe. His family stayed in the mission hospital bungalow, and he arranged for us to stay in another bungalow, three kilometres inside the forest.

As Sona prepared the evening meal, our sons Subodh and Sudhir played with the lid of a Coca Cola bottle. They started snatching it from one another. Sudhir put it in his mouth and suddenly it got stuck in his throat. He could not swallow it, nor could he vomit it out. He began to cry out loud. Sona and I tried to remove it. She put her finger in his mouth while I kept patting his back. With great difficulty, we took the lid out. But his mouth began to bleed and didn't stop. We didn't know what to do. It was utterly dark with no street lights. I took Sudhir on my shoulders, Sona took Subodh by the hand, and we walked to the Middleton's bungalow. We thank God that his wife, Helen, was a nurse. She immediately took Sudhir to the hospital and cared for him. After a few days, Sudhir was fine. In this way, God helped us in that difficult situation. To God be the glory!

6

Serving with Every Home Crusade

Instead, God chose things the world considers foolish in order to shame those who think they are wise. And he chose things that are powerless to shame those who are powerful (1 Corinthians 1:27).

Rev. M.M. Maxton

India Every Home Crusade, which began in October 1964, has its offices in different cities of India. After I completed the seminary course at Yavatmal, Maharashtra, we prayerfully waited for the Lord to open a door to serve Him. Then I received a letter from my close friend, Rev. M.M. Maxton, Director of India Every Home Crusade, Lucknow, UP. He wrote that IEHC had opened a new branch office at Jaipur, Rajasthan in April 1973. Dr. Anand Chaudhary, Director, Rajasthan Bible Institute served as Honorary Director temporarily. They were praying for a responsible and dedicated person to serve with IEHC at Jaipur. Rev. Maxton also said that he had already recommended me to the South Asia Director, Dr. B.A. Prabhakar.

"You can go and meet him in his office. The choice is yours," he said. When we returned to New Delhi, I met with Dr. B.A. Prabhakar at his office in Green Park. He clearly explained the vision of India Every Home Crusade in detail.

Dr. Jack McAllister

Founder and President of the World Literature Crusade, USA, Dr. Jack McAllister's vision was to spread the good news of the Gospel to every home, slum, and high society. This organisation is known as Every Home Crusade in every country except in America and Canada. Dr. B.A. Prabhakar said that we had embraced the vision and had merged with it. He offered me the responsibility to spread the Gospel door to door in the whole state of Rajasthan. One thing he made clear was that EHC was a faith ministry. We were not guaranteed any regular financial help.

"You will have full freedom to take the Good News through literature to each and every household, but you will also be accountable for each work and its accounts. If the Lord leads, you can be our co-worker."

On the way back, I shared with my wife what Dr. Prabhakar had explained to me. After seeking the Lord's will for two weeks, we had peace on this matter. We conveyed our decision to join this ministry with Dr. Prabhakar. We gave ourselves to the Lord completely with a fresh commitment.

Om the first day of June in 1973, we arrived in Jaipur with our family to serve with Every Home Crusade. I had the challenge of forming teams with the goal of taking the Gospel to every household in the entire state of Rajasthan by September 1975.

Workers for Harvest

Many young men came forward to join. We started from Banswada District on the border of Gujarat State. Bro. Thomas Paggi was made the team leader. We sent Gospel tracks systematically to every village. Bro. Cyril Cross from Allahabad, UP

Serving With Every Home Crusade

and then Bro. Prem Dayal from Kanpur, UP joined in the office to look after the follow-up. P.E. Bill Graham and Bro. Jagdhari Masih came to help with the Hindi correspondence and Bro. J.D. Baptist joined as an accountant. He was very responsible in his daily work. He was also a blessing to all who worked in the office and field. After that Bro. Satish Matthew came. Bro. Ummed Singh and one sister, Eliyama Ittee, joined us. She looked after the office correspondence. Other brothers and sisters also came to serve in the office and on the field. Though from different families, cultural and social backgrounds, churches and educational levels, we worked as one team. All contributed greatly according to their talents. By His grace, all accessible towns, villages, and slums of Rajasthan State were reached by the target time of September, 1975. It was a miracle indeed—praise the Lord!

In March 1980, the South Asia Director Dr. Prabhakar instructed me to shift to Chandigarh along with my family. After Bro. Marvin Pratap Singh from Southern Asia Bible College, Bangalore completed his Bible study, he

D. C. Kaushal with Evangelist Jaipur, Rajasthan

joined us in Jaipur. He was given the responsibility of follow-up works and did his work very well. He was encouraged to pursue his further studies while serving. Within a few years, this hardworking brother completed his B.D. and M.A. He was promoted to Office In-charge. When I was to be shifted from Jaipur to Chandigarh with my family, he was promoted to Office Manager. He was given the responsibility of Rajasthan's ministry because he was now experienced and well qualified. Later he was promoted to Assistant Director for Rajasthan.

Bro. Samuel Lal was a translator and teacher in a Christian School at Ajmer, Rajasthan. When I came to know about him, I called him from Ajmer to Jaipur and shared the vision of Every Home Crusade with him. After much prayer he decided to join us and was appointed as Office Manager in the Chandigarh office. Then in March 1985, the New Executive Director, Bro. B.A.G. Prasad, asked me to shift back to Jaipur along with my family as Bro. M.P. Singh had decided to serve with the Methodist Church in New Delhi. I was asked to close the Chandigarh office. It was a very painful experience for me.

Those who joined the ministry of EHC were full of zeal and passion to do the Lord's work. With full dedication, they served cheerfully and with commitment. Although some of the brothers among them were not well educated, they did not let this hinder them. Along with serving with EHC, some took the opportunity to improve their educational level as well. These brothers were inspired to improve their education standard because someone had encouraged and helped me to study further. It gave me such joy to see their growth. It is not an easy task to hand over your position to someone else. It is only possible by the grace of God. All those brethren were a blessing to me. All honour and glory to our only living God!

Deliverance

The meaning of the word "deliverance" in the Bible is varied. Whenever we talk about deliverance or being delivered, it clearly indicates that somebody is in bondage. Although we gained independence from the British nearly 70 years ago, the truth is that we are still in many kinds of bondages. Some are bound in sin; some are bound in curses. Some bondages are religious or economic. Some people are bound in thoughts; some are physically bound and some spiritually bound. We can be prisoners to strong emotions, tense relationships, or limited circumstances. There are many other kinds of bondages—caste, illiteracy, mental, loans, or poverty, for example.

The Lord knows the value of freedom. He does not want to see us in bondage. The Bible has many examples of the Lord Jesus delivering people who were oppressed. One such example is in the Gospel of Mark 5:1-20 and Luke 8:26-40.

> *So they arrived at the other side of the lake, in the region of the Gerasenes. When Jesus climbed out of the boat, a man possessed by an evil spirit came out from the tombs to meet him. This man lived in the burial caves and could no longer be restrained, even with a chain. Whenever he was put into chains and shackles—as he often was—he snapped the chains from his wrists and smashed the shackles. No one was strong enough to subdue him. Day and night he wandered among the burial caves and in the hills, howling and cutting himself with sharp stones.*
>
> *When Jesus was still some distance away, the man saw him, ran to meet him, and bowed low before him. With a shriek, he screamed, "Why are you interfering with me, Jesus, Son of the Highest God? In the name of God, I beg you, don't torture me!" For Jesus had already said to the spirit, "Come out of the man, you evil spirit." Then Jesus demanded, "What is your name?" And he replied, "My name is Legion, because there are many of us inside this man." Then the evil spirits begged him again and again not to send them to some distant place. There happened to be a large herd of pigs feeding on the hillside nearby. "Send us into those pigs," the spirits begged. "Let us enter them." So Jesus gave them permission. The evil spirits came out of the man and entered the pigs, and the entire herd of about 2,000 pigs*

plunged down the steep hillside into the lake and drowned in the water.

The herdsmen fled to the nearby town and the surrounding countryside, spreading the news as they ran. People rushed out to see what had happened. A crowd soon gathered around Jesus, and they saw the man who had been possessed by the legion of demons. He was sitting there fully clothed and perfectly sane, and they were all afraid. Then those who had seen what happened told the others about the demon-possessed man and the pigs. And the crowd began pleading with Jesus to go away and leave them alone.

As Jesus was getting into the boat, the man who had been demon possessed begged to go with him. But Jesus said, "No, go home to your family, and tell them everything the Lord has done for you and how merciful he has been." So the man started off to visit the Ten Towns of that region and began to proclaim the great things Jesus had done for him; and everyone was amazed at what he told them.

In a similar manner, Luke 13:10-17 talks about a woman with the spirit of infirmity. This woman went to the synagogue, but the ruler of the synagogue wouldn't even look at her. Another woman had an illness that caused bleeding for twelve years. She had spent all her resources on remedies but to no avail. The Israelites were slaves to the Egyptians for more than 430 years. Even after toiling hard, they were unable to satisfy their masters. All of them needed deliverance: some from evil spirits, some from illness, and some from slavery. The evil spirit-possessed man cried out day and night. Why? Possibly asking for deliverance.

The woman with the spirit of infirmity went to the synagogue with the hope that the priest would pray for the Lord to deliver her one day. The woman with the illness of bleeding for twelve years had spent everything, longingly looking to Jesus as a ray of hope. Israelites cried unto the Lord and the Lord heard them. In Exodus 3:8, He says, "So I have come down to rescue them from the power of the Egyptians..." He will initiate the deliverance. Hallelujah!

From the beginning of the world, there has been a big enemy of mankind, and we call him Satan. He deceived Adam and Eve so that they disobeyed God. As a result, man was bound in multiple ways and became a slave unto sin and Satan. Because of sin, man had to face death. Man was unable to do anything. Because of sin, it was impossible for man to have fellowship with the Holy God. He was unable to help himself.

The Bible says that God called out to the first man in the garden. "Adam! Where are you?"

Adam confessed his sin saying, "I hid from thee, O God, because I am naked." In other words, he said that I am here and he confessed about his naked state. He covered himself with leaves.

Today many people try to hide themselves with leaves or other unstable things. It is impossible to hide anything from the holy God. Since God is rich in His mercies, He planned to cover them with clothes. However, to fulfil this plan to give them clothes made of skin, the Lord had to sacrifice a blameless lamb and cover their nakedness with clothes made of its skin to forgive the sins of Adam and Eve.

For the deliverance of the Israelites, the blood of a blameless lamb was shed and was put on the doorpost of their houses. Those inside the houses were delivered. By wearing clothes, Adam could enter into the Lord's presence. The Bible tells us that all have sinned and fallen short of the glory of God. For this reason, God sent His only begotten Son Jesus (The Lamb) to give His life for all mankind (John 3:16). John the Baptist saw Jesus coming towards him and said, "Look! The Lamb of God who takes away the sin of the world!" (John 1:29) Today also the blood of Jesus (the Lamb of God) cleanses us from all our sins.

> *But if we confess our sins to him, he is faithful and just to forgive us our sins and to cleanse us from all wickedness* (1 John 1:9).

> *There is salvation in no one else! God has given no other name under heaven by which we must be saved* (Acts 4:12).

Let us see about the demon possessed man's deliverance and the life change he made that is mentioned in the Gospels according to Mark and Luke. We read that God answers three prayers. (See Mark 5:1-20 and Luke 8:26-40.)

1. The devil's confession and prayer: The devil saying "O Jesus, Son of the Most-High God" reflects that Satan also acknowledges who Jesus is, and he is accepting the power and lordship of Christ. The Lord God is almighty. Our God is a prayer answering God. Satan requested to send them among the herd of pigs and the Lord granted his prayer. What a merciful God we have. Hallelujah!

As soon as the evil spirits left the man, he became free. The man, who had been uncontrollable, became just like a new man. Being free from bonds is real deliverance. God today wants to deliver people from all kinds of bondages.

> *Then Jesus said, "Come to me, all of you who are weary and carry heavy burdens (bound, oppressed, possessed), and I will give you rest. Take my yoke upon you. Let me teach you, because I am humble and gentle at heart, and you will find rest for your souls"* (Matthew 11:28-29).

2. Prayer of the people: This event really shocked me. When people from neighbouring villages saw that this man was completely delivered from Satan's control and set free, they begged the Lord to depart from their region. Many were terrified by the powerful works of God. They became angry because of losing their 2,000 pigs. But the biggest problem of man is that he is unable to recognise the Lord Jesus. The Lifegiver came among them, but they knew Him not (John 1:10-11). The Lord Jesus heard their request and left the area.

3. Prayer of the delivered man: After his deliverance, the man eagerly wanted to be with the Lord. Now he didn't wander among the graves but had fellowship with the Lord. He was not naked but clothed. The Lord freely makes us righteous. When we wholeheartedly repent, seek forgiveness, and receive the Lord Jesus by faith as our Lord and Saviour, He forgives us and makes us righteous.

People who conceal their sins will not prosper, but if they confess and turn from them, they will receive mercy (Proverbs 28:13).

The Lord covers our nakedness of sin and clothes us with righteousness. When the formerly possessed man asked to go with Jesus, He told the man to go to his family and share the goodness of God. This is very important for the extension of the kingdom of the Lord and for the glory of God.

A long time ago, I heard a story from a servant of God regarding the preaching of the Gospel. A veterinarian was returning home in the evening after his work. Suddenly he heard a dog crying. Going further he saw a dog lying at the roadside, crying due to pain. Apparently a vehicle had driven over his leg and broken it. The doctor picked up the dog, took him to his home, and treated the dog. Though the leg healed, the dog stayed at the vet's house.

After a few years, the dog suddenly disappeared. The doctor

searched for him but couldn't find him. Some months later, a scratching at the door awakened the doctor from a deep sleep. The doctor got up and went to the door. Opening the door, he saw the same dog there. The doctor was very happy when the dog curled at his feet in love and probably asking for forgiveness. The doctor noticed another dog at the door that was unable to walk. Then the doctor understood that the first dog had brought the second dog there because he had been treated well and was healed there. Animals know where the one is who cares for them.

In the same manner, the Lord Jesus Christ also wanted the delivered man to go to those who were heavy laden, miserable, in slavery and without hope but waiting to be delivered, and tell them the great things God had done in his life. The Bible tells us that he went to the city and proclaimed God's great work and what He had done in his life. All the people were astonished. Some believe that this man preached throughout the ten cities of Decapolis and established churches.

Every man who has received new life by believing on the Lord has the responsibility to share his experience with those who are in darkness. They do not know who Jesus is.

This man's life was transformed. This was his proof of obedience towards his Deliverer.

> *The Lord Jesus after rising from the dead and before ascending to heaven, said to his eleven disciples, "I have been given all authority in heaven and on earth..." and He said unto them, "Therefore, go and make disciples of all the nations"* (Matthew 28:18-20).

Obedience is better than sacrifice.

It is my prayer that God would deliver our families, societies, and countries whose conditions are just like that of the demon possessed man. May the Lord Jesus break all bondages by the power of His blood. May the Lord be gracious so that every man who is delivered by the Lord Jesus would share his experience of salvation with others. Amen!

Similarly till July 1975, wherever it was possible, we tried to reach every household in Rajasthan to tell how one can receive new life and deliverance through Jesus Christ. For this work we formed a team of four to six young brothers. They were taught regarding discipleship during the first one week. We arranged some servants of God to come teach them. These included Rev. George Lukas, Ps. Thomas Matthews, Ps. M.K. Chacko, Ps. C.V. Roberts, Bro. Sarvanand Lal, Rev. M.M. Maxton, Rev. Anand Chaudhary and others.

Many churches, brothers and sisters among our states, helped us financially. Sister Lal from Nasirabad, Ajmer, Rajasthan also joined EHC, Jaipur. She encouraged people in the churches of Rajasthan, Punjab, and Haryana to support IEHC financially and through prayer.

An Unforgettable Incident

In August 1973, I was returning to Jaipur after visiting our first IEHC team in the Bagidora area of Banswada District. The last bus had already left for Udaipur City., and there were other people also with me. Since no transportation was available, we started walking. In a heavy downpour, five of us crossed the Mahi River on a broken bridge by holding the railing and walking by the side of the bridge. With great difficulty, we reached the other side.

After a couple of kilometres, we saw a police vehicle coming towards us. We motioned to them for help and the vehicle stopped. However, it was the Deputy Inspector General of Police (D.I.G.), Udaipur region, carrying his family. So we waited for other help but found none. A little while later, the same police vehicle returned. The driver was returning after dropping the family of the D.I.G. at a nearby village. We again motioned the vehicle to stop and pleaded with the driver, as he was returning to Udaipur city. With great difficulty, we persuaded the driver to give us a ride. Everything was fine until about 150 kilometres later when we reached Dungarpur. The vehicle came to a standstill in Khairwara village so we started pushing it. It started and then stopped. Again we pushed, and again it stopped. The same thing continued until 6:30 in the morning. Drenched by rain throughout the night, we arrived in Chetak Circle, Udaipur City.

I went to a nearby tea stall for a cup of tea. A programme titled Masihi Vandana (Back to the Bible) was being aired from Sri Lanka. Sipping my tea, I listened to Pastor Moti Lal preach. The pastor said that if we cast all our worries on the Lord, He cares for us. On hearing this word, I forgot all of my weariness. My heart filled with joy and peace. Our Lord Jesus is so wonderful! Praise His name!

Himmat Lal and the Village Chief

Evangelist Himmat Lal, who ministered in a village in Rajasthan, was dragged and brought before the village chief. A political group of young people had falsely accused him of stealing because they resisted his distribution of Gospel tracts in their village. A crowd gathered at the scene. Himmat Lal, in the presence of the village chief, spoke about the Lord Jesus and how the Lord had delivered him from all his sins. Impressed by Himmat Lal's words, the chief told the onlookers to go back to their homes. He wanted to know more. Himmat Lal then testified in great detail about the Lord Jesus Christ.

> *But before all this occurs, there will be a time of great persecution. You will be dragged into synagogues and prisons, and you will stand trial before kings and governors because you are my followers. But this will be your opportunity to tell them about me* (Luke 21:12-13).

Brother Guman Chand

A young man named Guman Chand listened intently as Himmat Lal talked to the village chief. On the way Guman Chand stopped Himmat Lal and expressed his desire to know more about Lord Jesus. Then Himmat Lal also testified to him in detail. On hearing the words of Himmat Lal, he accepted the Lord Jesus Christ. Guman's life was miserable, and there was no peace in the family. When Guman's family learned that he had accepted the Lord Jesus Christ, his wife and other family members thrashed him and threw him out of the home. From there he came to India Every Home Crusade, Jaipur office. Later he obeyed in the waters of baptism and started witnessing about the Lord. Today he continues to serve the Lord.

> *Let your conduct be without covetousness; be content with such things as you have. For He Himself has said, "I will never fail you. I will never abandon you"* (Hebrews 13:5).

Our team rented a house and worked in a small town in Rajasthan. On Sunday, while our brothers were worshipping the Lord, some people of that village gathered around the house. They persistently started knocking at the door. When the brethren opened the door, a young man vehemently punched Bro. Vardi Chand, spoke abusively and forced his way into the house. Others accompanied him. They beat our brethren so violently that their noses, ears, and mouths bled. Not only that, they forced them to leave the town. Our brothers packed their bags and went to the bus terminal. A crowd followed them and continued beating them until they boarded the bus for Jaipur.

This whole situation reminds me of the incident that happened with Peter and John, which is mentioned in the Bible:

> *So they called the apostles back in and commanded them never again to speak or teach in the name of Jesus* (Acts 4:18).

> *But those servants of God, instead of heeding their warning and in obedience to our Lord, continued to preach in the name of Jesus. Again, people captured and prison them, but an angel of the Lord delivered them out of prison. Even after suffering all this, the servants of the Lord thanked God saying they were counted worthy to suffer shame for His name's sake* (Acts 5:41b).

After this incident, Bro. Vardi Chand and Bro. Wilson were admitted to Sawai Mansingh Hospital. Their wounds healed, but marks of those injuries are still present on their bodies. An injury to Bro. Vardi's ear impairs his hearing to this day. We praise God that He saved the lives of our brothers that day!

Living Testimony—Kaleb Kerketta

I am the true grapevine, and my Father is the gardener. He cuts off every branch of mine that doesn't produce fruit, and he

Serving With Every Home Crusade

prunes the branches that do bear fruit so they will produce even more (John 15:1-2).

In January 1975, Masihdas Kerketta was serving with us. At that time we needed a driver for the ministry. Masihdas gave our address to his elder Bro. Kaleb. He came to our office in Jaipur. They had lost their parents in their early childhood and there was no one to look after them. Kaleb had many bad habits including paan (betel leaves prepared and used as a stimulant), tobacco, and alcohol. I was in the office when I heard a voice, "May I come in, sir?"

I saw a man standing at the door in a worn-out condition. I said to him, "Brother, please come in."

He had a strong smell of alcohol and I noticed a pack of beedi (cigarettes made of unprocessed tobacco and wrapped in leaves) and matchstick box in his pocket. His eyes were red. I asked him why he came.

"I am Masihdas Kerketta's elder Bro. Kaleb," he said. "He told me that you need a driver for the ministry."

"Do you drink?" I asked.

Yes sir," he replied politely. "I do drink and I am habitual to paan, beedi, and cigarette."

"Then, Brother, you are not able to join us. Such people cannot work here," I said.

"All right, then I will go back," he replied.

As he turned to leave, I heard a voice saying to stop him. I said, "Wait, Brother! I perceive that you have not come here on your own. The Lord must have some plans for you."

Then I called Bro. Satish, who worked in our office and said, "He is Masihdas's elder Bro. Kaleb. Take him to the guest room and ask him to take a bath. Meanwhile, please bring your shirt and pyjama and give it to him. Serve him tea and then ask him to sleep in the guest room. He needs rest."

Turning to Kaleb, I said, "Brother, please rest right now; we will talk in the evening." Later I told Bro. Satish and other brothers, "Come, we will pray for this brother that he may know the Lord personally and experience the Lord's love."

We prayed for him and Kaleb went to the guest room to sleep. When he woke up in the evening, Bro. Satish told him that the forgiveness of sins, true peace, and a blessing of new life is found only in Christ Jesus our Lord. Bro. Satish spent much time with him and prayed with him. That day Kaleb confessed his sins and gave his life to the Lord Jesus. It was evening and the office was closed. After giving him food, we left him alone in the guest room. I took the office keys and went home.

The next morning, I reached the office early. When I arrived at the gate, the landlord of our office waited for me outside.

"Pastor Ji, I heard someone crying the whole night in your office," he said. "We couldn't sleep last night, and we didn't have your telephone number to inform you. Who is inside? Who wept so bitterly all night?"

"Sir. Please wait here for a while; I will inquire and let you know," I said. I opened the office, went straight towards the guest room and called Kaleb.

"Jai Masih ki, sir!" answered Kaleb. His face radiated the glory of God and he smiled. He held me and cried. I also wept with him. He thanked me that I stopped him from going back home. I had never seen such a marvellous experience of life transformation. Even today I cannot forget that day; and whenever I get the opportunity, I often share about his dramatic change in my preaching.

During my fourteen years of service with India Every Home Crusade, many young people accepted the Lord and experienced genuine transformation. They served by my side; but such a life change of deliverance from sins and wickedness, I had never seen like Kaleb's. Glory to God!

Kaleb served with me for ten years from the Gujarat border to Kashmir's Leh-Ladakh during rain, scorching sun, storm, and freezing winters. He became a man of prayer and faithfulness and always ready to serve. How can I not speak about him? He was always ready to give his testimony near or far, wherever we stopped to minister. He happily gave his testimony of how the Lord changed his life. Currently he is serving the Lord independently at Jhansi.

"You are my witnesses" says the Lord (Isaiah 43:10).

Sukhram – S.R. Samuel

Instead, God chose things the world considers foolish in order to shame those who think they are wise. And he chose things that are powerless to shame those who are powerful. God chose things despised by the world; things counted as nothing at all, and used them to bring to nothing what the world considers important (1 Corinthians 1:27-28).

Needing young men to help complete the first coverage by September 1975, I contacted several Bible colleges and Bible schools in Rajasthan and other states. During the summer holidays, we invited their students to join us to take the good news to every home, so we could complete our work on schedule.

In this regards, I went to Bilaspur, Madhya Pradesh in February 1975 to visit the Bible seminary. I met with Principal Rev. Ishwari Lal and shared my purpose in coming to him. He gave me an opportunity to speak to students and challenge them with an opportunity to serve during their summer vacation. After thanking Rev. Ishwari Lal, I took a rickshaw to Bilaspur Railway Station.

About one kilometre before the railway station, I saw a barefooted young man about sixteen years old standing by the road distributing Gospel tracts. He shivered in the cold. As I approached, he took a tract from his shoulder bag and handed it to me. I stopped the rickshaw. Taking the tract from him, I asked, "Brother, who asked you to do this?"

In broken Hindi he replied, "Jesus has sent me!"

Hearing his reply, I was thrilled that a young man, despite his situation, was serving Christ. "Brother, what is your name, and where are you from?" I asked.

"Sir Ji, my name is Sukhram," he said. "I am from Kotpad village, Orissa State."

"How far educated are you?" I asked. He gestured that he had studied till fifth class.

"Do you want to learn more to serve more effectively?" I asked.

Nodding his head he said, "Yes!"

Then I introduced myself and asked, "Will you come with me to Jaipur, Rajasthan?" I saw a gleam of happiness in his eyes. After that he closed his eyes silently. Realising that he was praying, I told the rickshaw driver to wait for a while.

After ten minutes Sukhram replied, "Yes, sir! I will go with you."

"Brother, do you have more luggage with you?" I asked.

"Sir, this is all that I have," he replied.

How could he do such a thing unless the Lord Jesus is enthroned in his heart? I already had my return train ticket, so I purchased one for him. As we boarded the train, I told the ticket collector that this youth was with me. We rode in a single berth, covered by my blanket which I had taken for the journey. From Bilaspur we rode to Agra where we took a different train to Jaipur.

Serving With Every Home Crusade

After reaching Jaipur, I took Sukhram straight to my house and introduced him to my wife and children. I told them everything about him. After breakfast, we arranged for him to stay in the office. Gradually Bro. Sukhram started to work in the office. During the same time, I changed his name from Sukhram to S.R. Samuel. He was quite happy with his new name.

Bro. Samuel had a very good habit—whenever he had the time, he read his Bible and prayed. Every evening he took Gospel tracts on the street and the markets to preach the Gospel. I was so blessed by his life that I cannot express it in words. He did all his work gladly.

After three years, Bro. S.R. Samuel suddenly disappeared one day. We had no clue about where he had gone. We looked in various places but to no avail. I was very disturbed that we could not find this humble and cheerful believer.

On the third day of looking for him, one of a colleague asked, "Sir! Have you found out anything about Bro. Samuel?"

Taking a deep breath, I shook my head and said, "No."

"Sir, we have looked for our brother in all the places, but have not checked the basement of our office!" he said. "Who knows, our brother might be there!"

"Nobody would sit in the basement for such a long time." But I agreed that we should look for him there. The basement was where we kept all our literature. It was like a store. He went down into the basement and ran back upstairs. Terrified, he exclaimed, "Sir, Samuel is in the basement."

Surprised, I ran to the basement. Indeed, Samuel was there praying. He had poured sand over himself and had covered himself with a sack. Fearfully I called out, "Bro. Samuel! What are you doing here?"

"Sir, I am praying," he answered.

"Brother, we had been searching for you for a long time," I

said. "Why did you leave without telling us? Brother, you didn't even tell me that you were going for prayer."

"Sir, I didn't realise that I should inform you. I just come to prayer," he answered.

"Brother, why have you poured sand on yourself and put a sack on?"

Meekly he answered, "Even David put ashes on his head, wore sackcloths, and prayed by himself. I also prayed by myself to God likewise."

My heart was overjoyed. Embracing him, I thanked the Lord for this brother. "Brother, what is the matter that you came here to pray? If there is any problem, please share it with me. We will also pray."

"Sir, I want to serve in my region of Orissa," he said. "This is a very good thing." All of the colleagues present in the office prayed and thanked the Lord for him.

After some time, he joined the Bible course at Rajasthan Bible Institute, Jaipur. Thereafter, Samuel went to Orissa to serve the Lord. By this time, he had learned to speak and understand the Hindi language. This young man, who dedicated his complete life to serve the Lord, amazed me. I often remember and pray for him.

Within a short time, he established about 100 home fellowships in villages and small prayer fellowship groups. Today, he joyfully serves the Lord with his whole family. Indeed, if this kind of committed life and prayer warriors are found in every believer's families, in churches, villages, or tribal regions, transformation will surely take place. Amen!

> *Even before he made the world, God loved us and chose us in Christ to be holy and without fault in his eyes. God decided in advance to adopt us into his own family by bringing us to himself through Jesus Christ. This is what he wanted to do, and it*

gave him great pleasure. So we praise God for the glorious grace he has poured out on us who belong to his dear Son. He is so rich in kindness and grace that he purchased our freedom with the blood of his Son and forgave our sins (Ephesians 1:4-7).

When I heard that our team had been attacked and brutally beaten by an anti-Christian group, I traveled to Chittaurgarh, Rajasthan to see their situation. When we passed the large industrial city of Bhilwara, I started thinking we should have an English school there. I felt we could help at least one or two evangelists financially, and that our financial burden would also be reduced. At the same time Christian brothers and sisters would get an opportunity to work.

Finally we started a school at Bhilwara but without getting permission from the leadership. We named it Saint Paul School. I informed all my leaders about this good work during the Bangalore Conference. They objected and I had to submit to the leadership of IEHC.

We started this school with eleven students. Some teachers were Christians from Ajmer and two teachers were from UP. Soon the numbers of students increased and, after some time, the school had 375 students. After prayer, we handed the responsibility of the school over to a young widow, Mrs. Joyce Prasad, who had two children. She was a well qualified teacher. Bro. John Shashi Anand was appointed as the school manager.

Struggle of Dhaniram

I say then: Walk in the Spirit, and you shall not fulfil the lust of the flesh (Galatians 5:16).

This is the story of the struggles of a young man Dhaniram, who spent fifteen days with me. To hide his identity, I have changed his name and so will address him as Dhaniram.

When Dhaniram came to the faith, he was studying in High School and was from a low cast family. He found a Gospel booklet on the road and read it, anxious to know more. Later he met a preacher whom he asked about Jesus. The preacher shared everything in detail about Jesus Christ and told him that, on believing in Christ, we receive forgiveness from all kind of sins. He said that regardless of how our sins are—black, red, yellow, dirty, stench filled and disgusting—the Lord Jesus can deliver us from them all.

After listening to all this, Dhaniram said, "My life is very dirty."

The preacher asked, "How dirty?"

He replied, "I have done all kind of fornication, not only this, I have done disgusting things with girls and married women. How can the Lord Jesus forgive a person like me?"

The preacher said, "Look, Brother, our Lord Jesus Christ can forgive every kind of sin. He took all your sins upon Himself on the cross and freed you from all your sins and curses by shedding His blood on cross. He loves you. If you confess your sins and trust him, then He will surely forgive you.

> *Jesus said Come unto me, all ye that labour and are heavy laden, and I will give you rest. Take my yoke upon you, and learn of me; for I am meek and lowly in heart: and ye shall find rest unto your souls* (Matthew 11:2-29).

> *If we confess our sins, he is faithful and just to forgive us our sins, and to cleanse us from all unrighteousness* (1 John 1:9).

Listening to the words of the preacher, he confessed his sins and found comfort in his life. It was a miracle. Hallelujah!

After these things, this brother came in contact with me. It was already more than two or more yearsbsince he had believed on the Lord, and I was only a two-month-old believer.

Serving With Every Home Crusade

Sometimes he would share some small things about his life and ask, "Brother, I cannot find victory over these things. I still do these things in secret."

I would encouraged him to be patient and walk in the leading of the Holy Spirit. He opened every aspect of his life before me. Perhaps the reason for our close friendship was that we were both from Hindu family background and different villages. After about two months, he disappeared.

Then after 25 years, suddenly he knocked at my door. During the conversation, he told me that he was still unmarried but, during those years, he had relations with several women. Then he began to cry, saying that despite his unwillingness, he fell prey to sin again and again. He wanted to know what he should do.

I replied, "Brother, I do not have any solution for this. Except the Lord, no one can help in this matter. Only by the help of the Lord and His blood, you can have victory over these things." I shared some scripture portions like Romans 3:23 and 6:23, Psalms 32 & 51, Isaiah 1:17-18 and prayed. Be patient with yourself and be glad in the Lord. I counselled and helped him the best I could.

Then he said, "Sometimes I get very angry at myself. I cannot become a good Christian. Thoughts of suicide come to my mind."

I was shocked and asked, "How does it come to your mind?"

He said, "No one except me can understand the ongoing conflict within me. Others perceive me as a good man, but only I know what's inside." Then he said, "Okay! Can you help me, I want to get married!"

I asked him to improve his education, and then I would help him. I comforted him and took him with me. I made it clear to him to stay in discipline, to grow in the Word, and have a prayer life. "Your life must transform," I said. Then he began to serve with me.

A week later, he disappeared again, and I did not know where he was. I felt very sorry. It appeared that he was possessed by many sexual evil spirits, which were driving him astray, like the man in Mark 5:1-21.

I had to go to the city for some important work. One day I met Dhaniram distributing tracts, and I recognized him. He seemed very changed. There was a glow on his face. After meeting, we both were happy. I sensed that Dhaniram was delivered from his bondages, but I did not discuss those things.

He expressed his joy to meet me, "Bro. Kaushal, I am very very thankful to the Lord for true deliverance. Now I share a transparent relationship with God. Thank you for your friendship. I have been victorious over all the bondages by the power of God and the blood of Jesus. He is my Redeemer and Deliverer. I have experienced true peace by His grace. He has washed me totally with His blood and gave me victory over all my problems."

I believe that the Lord must have spoken to him in His own way. Hallelujah!

But Jesus looked at them and said, "With men it is impossible, but not with God; for with God all things are possible" (Mark 10:27).

D.C. Kaushal with South Asia Director and staff

7

Door to Door Visiting Jammu and Kashmir

For the Lord gave us this command when he said, "I have made you a light to the Gentiles, to bring salvation to the farthest corners of the earth" (Acts 13:47).

Starting in October 1976, I carried the additional responsibility of the Chandigarh Office. This included the states of Himachal, Jammu-Kashmir, Leh-Ladakh, Haryana, Punjab, and Chandigarh Union Territory. From April 1980 to March 1983, we delivered the message of salvation from house to house in these states.

In 1983, the Lord gave us the privilege to serve in the northern states of Jammu and Kashmir, a very challenging and an unforgettable experiences. According to His promises, the Lord never left or forsook us. I would like to share some incidents that occurred during our ministry in Jammu and Kashmir.

Jehovah Jireh

Abraham named the place Jehovah-Jireh (which means "the Lord will provide"). To this day, people still use that name as a proverb: "On the mountain of the Lord it will be provided" (Genesis 22:14).

While serving in Jammu & Kashmir, we had twelve teams engaged in track distribution. One team had six young men. They had joined us from many different states including Uttar Pradesh, Madhya Pradesh, Karnataka, Gujarat, Rajasthan, Orissa, Andhra Pradesh, and Maharashtra. We rented a house in Jammu City and made it our base. From there it was easy to care for our teams, providing the literature and financial help quickly.

During that time we faced financial problems. It became a challenge for us to meet their daily needs such as food, supplies, rent, and transportation. We started receiving calls from various teams, saying, "Sir, the month has ended. Our money is exhausted. Now the landlord has also started asking for rent. There is nothing for food. We are desperately in need of money. Please send us some money. It is a very difficult time."

But the truth was that we had no money. What could we do? We called the finance director Bro. Robert Luis in Bangalore, explained our financial situation to him, and requested that he send monetary help as soon as possible.

"We do not have funds to send you," he replied.

I requested a second time and told him about our situation.

"I would urge you to pray," he answered.

"Brother, we are praying," I said.

During our morning devotion time the next day, the office staff was present. We presented this situation before them and asked for special prayers. Bro. Samuel H. Lal opened his Bible and encouraged everyone by reading from Isaiah 37:1-5. We continued to lift the entire situation to God in prayer.

After four days, our office door bell rang, and Bro. Satish Matthew went to the door. A postman stood there and handed an urgent envelope to him. Bro. Satish saw that the sender was the finance director. He immediately took the envelope to our accountant, Bro. Sushil Peter. When he opened the envelope, he saw that a bank draft of Rs. 27,500/= was enclosed. Immediately he came and told us what was in the envelope. We were amazed and praised the Lord.

> *The Lord is my shepherd; I have all that I need* (Psalm 23:1).

> *Even strong young lions sometimes go hungry, but those who trust in the Lord will lack no good thing* (Psalm 34:10).

The Lord answered our prayers and met our needs in His time. Just as David also said, "In my desperation I prayed, and the Lord listened; he saved me from all my troubles" (Psalm 34:6). All of us rejoiced, pouring out heartfelt thankfulness, and praised God for all His mercies.

> *Taste and see that the Lord is good. Oh, the joys of those who take refuge in him!* (Psalm 34:8)

> *Let them offer sacrifices of thanksgiving and sing joyfully about his glorious acts* (Psalm 107:22).

> *I will praise the Lord at all times. I will constantly speak his praises* (Psalm 34:1).

Attention Gone; Accident On!

> *So let us come boldly to the throne of our gracious God. There we will receive his mercy, and we will find grace to help us when we need it most* (Hebrews 4:16).

This incident took place on a fine day in June 1983 when we were serving in Jammu and Kashmir. My family was staying with our team there. I drove to the market to buy fruit and other groceries. After buying the food, I put them on the front seat next to me. On the way back, I realised that the paper bag was tearing apart and fruit were falling out. I reached over to pick up the fruit. By taking my attention off the road, I caused an accident.

I don't know how a man came to be under the car, but holding the car bumper, that man was dragged with the car quite far. When people saw this they shouted, so I stopped the car at the side. I alighted from the car and gasped when I saw a man under the car. A crowd gathered instantly. But by God's grace, he had suffered only minor scratches. By this time the police came and took me to a nearby police station. The D.I.G. Police of Jammu region was visiting the police station. While entering the gate he met me at the front of porch and asked, "What is the matter?"

"Sir!" I replied. "I am a Christian and, because of my mistake, this man came under the car."

He looked at that man and asked, "Are you okay?"

"Yes sir," he answered. "I suffered slight scratches only."

"From now on, be careful while driving," the officer said to me.

Then he turned to the man, "Go and get some treatment."

I left from there with a grateful heart and thanking the Lord. This was a miracle of God because it was not a small accident. Even though he was caught under the car, this man did not suffer any major injuries. Also, the D.I.G. officer in the police station was merciful, asking me to leave with only a warning. All of this was the mercy of God and a good lesson for me.

I treasure such countless miracles in the corner of my heart always and thank the Lord for His love, grace and deliverance. The Word of the Lord also says that,

> Let all that I am praise the Lord; may I never forget the good things he does for me (Psalm 103:2).

I make it my habit to remember the Lord's help and to always give thanks to Him. After this incident, I stopped driving the car.

The Difficult Journey to Leh-Ladakh

The political conditions were not favourable in Jammu and Kashmir. Dr. Farooq Abdullah's government was overthrown by Prime Minister Mrs. Indira Gandhi on July 1, 1983. There was a total strike, and no mode of transportation was available. A group of our co-workers and other brothers were staying at Rev. Jonathan Pauljor's guest house in Srinagar, Kashmir. We needed to travel from there to Leh-Ladakh the next day. We learned that some trucks, loaded with groceries and vegetables, were about to leave for Leh-Ladakh so we boarded the two trucks.

When we reached about 14,000 feet elevation, we all had much difficulty breathing. At Jojula Pass, I was almost unconscious because of the lack of oxygen. We had not adequately prepared for this problem. My condition continued to deteriorate so Bro. Sanand Lohia tearfully prayed for me. His tears fell on my cheeks. I thanked God that He quickly answered his prayer and instantly I felt completely well.

It was almost night near Kargil when the driver stopped the truck. He left us by the roadside in the freezing cold. Saying that he would be back soon, he went to the nearby village. The night was unbearably cold, and we could hardly sleep. The Lord kept us alive through the night. Early the next morning, the driver returned. The second night of the trip, we stayed in a lodge on the banks of the Dras River. The third day, we arrived in Leh-Ladakh around 4 o'clock in the evening and stayed at the Moravian Memorial School, Leh.

Sharing the Gospel in Leh-Ladakh

So faith comes from hearing, that is, hearing the Good News about Christ (Romans 10:17).

The Moravian missionaries came at the beginning of the eighteenth century and did a big missionary work there. Along with the graves of the missionaries, were graves of their little children. Some of the graves of these missionaries have disappeared. We recognised the dedication by which these missionaries served. The pastor told us that these missionaries struggled greatly for the name of our Lord, suffering much pain. Leaving their own country, families, language, and foods, they lived among these mountain people, learned their language, and served the Lord. Because of their hard work, the people listened to the Gospel and accepted Christ. Small Christian groups can be found in the Leh-Ladakh region.

While the Gospel was being delivered in the Leh-Ladakh areas of Jammu Kashmir, Bro. Subodh Kumar and Bro. Walter Masih had an opportunity to deliver the Gospel to the people from house to house in Janskar Valley, located at the northeast region of Kargil. That area has many Buddhist monasteries. These brothers walked on icy paths to present the Gospel in the regions about 15,000 above sea level. Except for mules, there is no mode of transportation to reach these cold places.

These brothers spent the nights in tents set up for travellers and tourists. After visiting homes in the valley one night, they spotted a snow leopard wandering around their tents. It seemed ferocious as if he were about to attack. They prayed, trusting the Lord to save them. After sometime, the leopard left. The Lord protected the lives of our bretheren. Praise be to God!

Opposition from Muslim Fundamentalists

For the Lord loves justice and he will never abandon the godly. He will keep them safe forever, but the children of the wicked will die (Psalm 37:28).

Our brothers were serving in Kishtwar town where they rented a house. Every morning they carried their bags full of Gospel tracts and went to the villages one by one. Their landlord and his wife were good to them. They feared God and treated our brothers very well.

During that time, the Muslim fundamentalist groups opposed our brothers and threatened to make them leave, or else the consequences could be worse. Their landlord had a small business. The Muslim fundamentalists also threatened the landlord, saying that, if he did not evict these people by evening, they would burn their house.

I did them no wrong, but they laid a trap for me. I did them no wrong, but they dug a pit to catch me (Psalm 35:7).

When two brothers returned early before the others, the situation became tense. The fundamentalists slowly started to gather outside the house. The two brothers were stuck with no way to escape. They feared that the fundamentalists would find them in the house and surely drag them out to kill them. The landlord's family hid the two brothers in a big tin box in which they stored their winter clothes and heaped more clothes on top. It looked as though the clothes had been lying there for a long time. The fundamentalists searched the whole house, every nook and corner of each room, but they found nothing. "Where are those men?" they asked the landlord.

"They have already left," he replied. All thanks be to God, that their attention did not go to that box. Our brothers had kept silent. After finishing the search and being fully satisfied that no one was there, they left. Later the whole atmosphere calmed down.

At that time, I was with Pastor Jonathan in Srinagar. The brothers, who had not reached the house but were outside, called Pastor Jonathan on the phone and informed him about this whole incident. I assured them that I would be there as soon as possible and asked them to pray. I rented a jeep, arrived there by night, rescued the two brothers who were trapped there, and brought them back to Srinagar the same night.

It was the Lord's great miracle that those two brother's lives were saved. Who knows what would have happened to them if they had been found by the fundamentalists. But by God's mercy, the landlord and family acted very wisely in protecting those brothers. Praise the Lord!

There are many such incidents like this; some of them are beyond explanation. This task of preaching the Gospel was a team work, which was led by the Holy Spirit. The wondrous thing is that during those four months of ministering in Kashmir, none of the brethren got sick. The brothers were very excited about the work. They had only one goal—to reach every home with the glorious Gospel of the Lord Jesus. To achieve it they walked, cycled, and rode buses and even mules. Jammu

Kashmir has three major regions. Jammu has a majority of Hindu people and these people speak Hindi, Urdu, and Dogri. The Kashmir region, constituted mostly of Muslims, speak Urdu and the Kashmiri language. The Leh-Ladakh people, who are mostly Buddhists, speak the Ladakhi language. However, they also understood Hindi. Our brothers belonged to different regions with different languages, but these brethren reached them with the glorious Gospel in spite of their varied daily routines, cultures, languages, and food habits. They were not disappointed or dismayed. They had brotherly love among them. They had the spirit of forgiveness. They were prayer warriors. None of them were perfect, but they grew in love and respect for each other. They were all equal in Christ Jesus. This reflects the first century Church.

Christ-Group Formation

We distributed two kinds of tracts—one for the children and the other for adults. Because our office address was printed on them, people contacted us. After reading the tracts, they wanted to know more about the Lord Jesus. In response, we mailed to them a Bible study course, "The Way to a Happy Life." We also gave certificates to them on completion of the course. Many still write to us, desiring to know more and more about the Lord. We conducted meetings at special venues near them to which they could easily travel. They asked questions and we provided answers. Men and women from various walks of life participated—common people, students, doctors, engineers, and businessmen. Those who acknowledged their sins and accepted the Lord Jesus as their personal Saviour came for a time of prayer, worship, and reading from the Word. We called them the Christ-Group. This ministry spread across many places.

I had the privilege in hosting Dr. Dick Eastman, First School of Prayer at YMCA, New Delhi, along with Rev. C. George. Now he is the president of Every Home For Christ International, based in Colorado, USA.

The Lord chose simple men and anointed them to lead. This ministry grew like the early church as described in the Acts of the Apostles. They faced resistance but never backed down from testifying for the Lord. This was a very blessed ministry and was soon established in several places in the Punjab and Rajasthan. Even today, many Christ-Groups are being established all over India. Rev. C. George was the National Christ-Group Director, based at Delhi. Later his office moved to Kerala State.

Rev. C. George (National Director – Christ Group) with Christ Group Leaders

While walking with the Lord, my journey has been very blessed. Memories of serving alongside my IEHC colleagues include both bitter and sweet experiences. These have taught me many lessons about faith and Christian character. The following are ome of my experiences.

A Bitter Root—Anger

Look after each other so that none of you fails to receive the grace of God. Watch out that no poisonous root of bitterness grows up to trouble you, corrupting many (Hebrews 12:15).

Door to Door Visiting Jammu and Kashmir

This incident happened at the beginning of 1982 when we lived in Chandigarh. I was with Every Home Crusade, serving in the areas of Himachal Pradesh, Punjab, Haryana, Jammu & Kashmir. For Sunday worship, we attended the Church of Chandigarh. The owners of the church property were Mr. and Mrs. Dhillon. One day the couple came to visit us and asked if I could help them in their church ministry. Their pastor had resigned, and there was no one else to lead. I told them that, without official permission, I could not consent to it. I wrote to my South Asia Director, Rev. Prasad, on this matter and asked for his guidance. In response to my letter, Rev. Prasad said, "If you have time, you can help them. But your first priority is IEHC."

Then I replied to the Dhillons, and they entrusted the church responsibilities to me in 1982. During Easter Week that year, I invited and arranged for a servant of God from Delhi to speak. Some people accepted the Lord in the meeting, many were blessed, and seven were baptised. Our son Subodh John was among them. After the Easter Sunday service, lunch was served. Then I went to drop the speaker off at the Chandigarh bus terminal. As I returned home, the phone was ringing. Mr. Dhillon was on the phone, asking me to come to him immediately. I arrived at his home and he opened the door and stood in the doorway.

"Brother Ji, you called me?" I asked. "What is the matter?"

"Yes! I called you," he said sternly. "Vacate our premises today!"

I was shocked. I could not understand it. I asked, "Brother Ji, what happened?"

"He said, get out!" he shouted. His wife stood behind him. With tears in her eyes, she nodded in agreement with her husband for me to leave.

I was confused. I didn't know what had gone wrong or who had done back biting. After returning home, I told my wife Sona the whole matter. The biggest problem was that he asked us to vacate that day. It was already three o'clock in the afternoon. Our office was on their ground floor, and the church was above it on first floor.

We had to go in the evening to a friend's house. His wife was the principal of a nursing college. Due to our circumstances, we were not in the mood to go; but since they called us with so much love, we went in the evening. As soon as we reached their house, they were standing on the porch and welcomed us warmly.

Bro. Cherian apparently read my anxiety and problems. His wife took my wife and the kids inside. The brother grabbed my hand and asked me, "Pastor Ji, what happened? You seem upset. Something has happened. Please tell me what happened. What can I do for you?"

I could not control myself and told him everything.

"Oh! This is it!" He took me in his washroom and asked me to wash my face. "Take care of yourself. I'll be back."

Bro. Cherian immediately went to his neighbour, Dr. Sharma, who owned a house that had been vacant several months. "Is your house still available for rent?" he asked.

"Yes! It is available," said Dr. Sharma. "But for whom do you want it?"

"Our Pastor Ji needs it," replied Bro. Cherian. Dr. Sharma immediately gave him the keys of his house, without even asking who Pastor Ji was, his name, which place they hail from, or what he would do in the house. Bro. Cherian even helped us moved from the church to Dr. Sharma's house. I'm very thankful for our Bro. Cherian. In reality, God gave us more than we could ask for.

Door to Door Visiting Jammu and Kashmir

I will answer them before they even call to me. While they are still talking about their needs, I will go ahead and answer their prayers! (Isaiah 65:24)

We vacated the other premises by 10:30 pm that same night. The next morning I went to the Dhillon's home and gave him the keys. He asked, "Have you vacated?"

"Yes Brother!" I said.

Mrs.Dhillon, who was a prayerful sister, continued to visit our house for about six months. She was like an elder sister, or more like a mother to me. Whenever she visited, she would say, "Brother, please forgive us."

But the bitterness had rooted deep down in my heart. One day with courage I told her, "Sister Ji, I am not able to forgive. I do not know why this is so." During those six months, my spiritual life had turned completely hollow. I had no rest, no peace. I became like a piece of wood infected with termites. I was defeated and beaten. The Christian community considered me as a spiritual leader, co-worker, disciple and prayer warrior. Inwardly my condition was different. I was living a hypocritical life.

One of my friends Pastor B.L. Prem was serving in the Church of North India in Chandigarh. He was a very simple natured, Spirit-filled servant of God and a good friend of mine. One day during our conversation, he said, "Brother, do you know of any preacher? Our church is planning for a Gospel meeting."

I suggested Bro. Tony from Lucknow, UP. He agreed instantly, so I invited Bro. Tony to preach as I had good relations with him. Bro. Tony came and the meetings began. On the second day of the meeting, while he was preaching, he looked towards me from the stage and said, "How long will you nurse this bitterness? You have already become hollow! Ruined your spiritual life! God wants you to remove this problem." Then he quoted,

Leave your gift there before the altar, and go your way. First be reconciled to your brother, and then come and offer your gift (Matthew 5:23-24).

Like a sudden bolt of lightning striking within, each incident that had occurred in recent months emerged one after another before my eyes. I felt heaviness inside. I knew that something was inadvertently not right. Maybe I had unknowingly hurt the Dhillons by not sharing that I had invited a brother from New Delhi for the Passion Week service.

Burdened in the Spirit, I could not bear that heaviness any more. I needed to apologise. I got up in the middle of the Gospel meeting and went straight to Mr. Dhillon's house. I earnestly apologised. "Please forgive me. I must have done something wrong;that's why you did this to me." And thus, I restored my relationship with him. After this I felt very light within. A treasured joy that I had lost was now restored.

By this incident, I learned to never hold any bitterness against any brother or sister in my heart. I did all this so that there would be no hindrance in my relationship with the Lord. Those six months of my life had been extremely difficult and painful. Thank God that He enabled me to ask for forgiveness from the Dhillons and to forgive myself. Whether Mr. Dhillon forgave me or not, it did not matter. I had done my part ,and my conscience was clear before the Lord. Hallelujah!

New Vision

While living in Chandigarh, I was responsible for I.E.H.C. ministry for the whole north-west of Indian (Punjab, Haryana, Rajasthan, Himachal Pradesh and Jammu and Kashmir). On 1st March 1985, I traveled by bus to Delhi on an invitation from The Bible Society of India, New Delhi. I was to attend the

Door to Door Visiting Jammu and Kashmir

launching ceremony for the new translation of the Punjabi language Bible. The first copy of the Bible in the Punjabi language was to be presented to President Gianni Jail Singh at Rashtrapati Bhavan.

On the way, I saw a vision of a map of Delhi on the screen of the bus. The northeastern part of the map was white, while the northwest part was black. With this vision, I heard a clear voice, "Go, and preach the Gospel to the black area." The next day after taking part in the launching ceremony of the Punjabi Bible, I returned back to Chandigarh. First, I shared the vision with my wife. "You are already in service of the Lord, what else do you want?" she replied pessimistically. On receiving a negative response from my wife, I started to seriously focus on the vision of the Lord and spent time in prayer to know if it was of the Lord.

I received an invitation from Rev. Y.D. Jayaseelan to participate in meetings he had arranged with Pastor Peter Yangrin in New Delhi in March 1985. The theme of the message on the first day was "Vision." Pastor Peter Yangrin spoke. The second day was "Faith," the third day the subject was "The Great Commission," and the fourth day the message was on "Obedience." In four days, I felt as if Pastor Peter Yangrin was speaking to me only. I realised that the Lord was making clear the vision.

While in my personal prayer time and meditation, I already knew that this vision was from the Lord. The Lord had called me to a new place to serve Him. Now it was my turn that I should obey Him and leave the rest in His hands. Being excited by this new step, I shared with Bro. C. George, National Christ-Group Director, in New Delhi. He said, "You wait for some time and pray about it. Maybe the Lord might send somebody else for this work."

After this, I shared my vision with my very close friend and brother, Rev. M.M. Maxton, Director, IEHC, Lucknow, UP. His response was, "How can you do this? Your children are still studying and the time for their marriage will approach soon! What about your retirement? Who will help your children?" He further said, "Think about it again."

Meanwhile, South Asia Director Mr. B.A.G. Prasad asked me in the last week of March 1985 to move to Jaipur, Rajasthan on April 1, 1985 and to close the Chandigarh office. Bro. M.P. Singh, Assistant Director of I.E.H.C. in Rajasthan, had resigned and wanted to serve in New Delhi.

My wife was a little confused. The decision was very shocking for us. Our children were studying in Chandigarh, and we were concerned about how they would get admission to the school at Jaipur. Our son Subodh John was studying in a government college with only one more year left to complete. But I accepted the decision of my leaders, as my Pastor M.K. Chacko had taught me saying, "Obey those who are over you, and be submissive. God will bless you." Though it was painful, we obeyed. Praise the Lord!

8

Miracle in New York

Don't be afraid, for I am with you. Don't be discouraged, for I am your God. I will strengthen you and help you. I will hold you up with my victorious right hand (Isaiah 41:10).

In July 1985, I went to America to take part in a South Asia Mission Conference and for promotional work with Every Home for Christ International. After the conference, I worked with EHC International in the promotional department in different states. Upon returning, I went to meet my friend in New York. I had met him during the revival meetings held for a week at Calvary Camps in Ashland, Virginia. He had urged me to spend some time with him before returning to India. I had to confirm my return ticket with the Alitalia Airlines office in New York. My friend was quite busy with his work, so he asked his friend Alex to help me. Bro. Alex accompanied me to the airline office.

We got my air ticket confirmed. When we came out of the office, I noticed that it was snowing lightly. I watched snow fall for the first time in my life. At first, I enjoyed it. As we walked a little further, I started feeling cold because I was wearing only a sweater. Bro. Alex gave me his overcoat, but still I felt chilled. We went to a nearby KFC Restaurant to have tea and wait for the snow to stop. While we were sitting there, I put my handbag on a chair next to me. The bag had my passport, confirmed return air ticket, and $1,700, which the believers of the various churches had given to me as personal gifts.

We talked over tea and enjoyed watching the weather outside. Suddenly I turned toward my bag and saw that it was missing. I was shocked! Some black (Afro-American) youth sat behind us, making a lot of noise. My friend Alex cried when he learned that my bag had disappeared. We immediately went to the manager of the restaurant and told him about the missing bag. The manager insisted that he knew nothing about it. My friend suspected that the manager was not telling the truth.

Bro. Alex took me to a nearby police station to inform the police of our situation. We prayed that they could help us. The police told us clearly that my passport could be recovered, but the rest of the articles and the money were impossible to get back. Possibly the thief had thrown away what was useless to him in a nearby garbage can. They registered my complaint and gave me a copy of the FIR (First Information Report).

We took the FIR copy to the Alitalia Airlines office. After learning about the whole event, the staff said that I had to buy another oneway air ticket, and then they would issue my ticket. I had no money at all. I persisted in asking them to help me. They suggested that I contact my travel agent in India and ask him to fax all the details of my ticket and passport. Then they could issue another ticket to me.

With Bro. Alex's help, I called my travel agent in New Delhi, India, and informed him of my situation in detail. I asked him to send all the necessary information of my return ticket to Alitalia Airlines office by fax as soon as possible. My agent, who was a believer, advised me to stay calm and assured me of his quick help.

Alex invited me to go with him to his home. He informed his wife, Laurie, about the situation, and we three start praying with one accord. That night I stayed at Alex and Laurie's home.

Miracle in New York

Alex was from Puerto Rico. He spoke Spanish and had served in Brooklyn, New York, for quite some time. His wife was born in New York and spoke good English. They had married a year before. Here in New York, they served among the Spanish speaking people. I was having considerable difficulty in understanding Alex's broken English, but Sister Laurie explained what he said to me. It was a strange experience! But the Lord Jesus has been my Helper in all circumstances.

The next day the three of us went to the Indian Consulate Office in New York City. Alex and Laurie prayed in a corner side as I also prayed while standing in line. When my turn came, I gave a copy of the police complaint to the officer and explained my situation to him. The first question that the officer at the consulate asked, "Do you have any proof that you are an Indian?"

"Yes sir, I am an Indian!" I replied.

He started laughing and then said, "Hello Mister! We need a proof."

"I am telling you sir! I am an Indian," I said.

"Do you have any valid document that proves you are a citizen of India?" he asked. "Do you have any letters that any of your friends might have written to you in India before coming here, asking you to bring something from here?"

I remembered that I had a letter in my briefcase from Bro. M.M. Maxton. He had written to me before I left Jaipur in which he had given me information about the U.S.A. and suggested that I be careful in New York. I also had an invitation letter from the General Secretary, Dr. D. John Richard of E.F.I., which he had given me to attend a South Asia Mission Conference in California. I handed both letters to the officer. By those documents, the officer believed that I was a citizen of India. "Where do you live in India?" the officer asked.

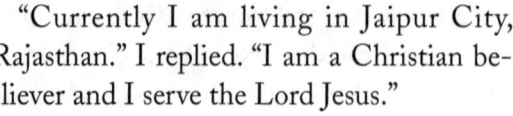

"Currently I am living in Jaipur City, Rajasthan." I replied. "I am a Christian believer and I serve the Lord Jesus."

"Okay! You can come on Monday."

"Sir, I have to return to India on Monday," I said. "Please issue me a duplicate passport."

"This is not possible," he replied. "This process takes time."

"Please help me," I implored. "I have neither a relative nor any close friend in this country. I am completely helpless here."

Throughout this time, Alex and Laurie prayed continuously. The Lord touched this officer's heart and he said, "All right! Please wait for a while." Twenty-five minutes later, the officer called me and handed me a new passport that was valid for one month only. Thanking him, I returned to Alex and Laurie and told them about everything that happened. We rejoiced, praising God exuberantly together. Hallelujah!

With grateful hearts, we headed towards the Alitalia office for my ticket. We were walking on air. The Lord was teaching us to rejoice in the festivities of victory.

We went straight to the ticket confirmation counter and told the lady at the counter about all that had happened at the Indian Consulate office. "Our Lord did a miracle there and we believe He will also do one here."

The woman sitting at the counter said, "Your Lord must have worked there, but here it is impossible."

"Okay. Please start working on my ticket. Our Lord Jesus Christ can make the impossible into possible."

She stood up and went into the office blabbering something, and we began to pray in front of the reception desk.

About 45 minutes later she returned with a white paper

swinging in her hand. "We just received all the information from your travel agent about your ticket and passport." Smiling, she issued my air ticket and handed it over to me without any charges. Then she said, "What happened today has never happened before. Truly, your God can do amazing things!"

When I asked her name, she said, "My name is Lucy, and I am a Jew." Then we prayed for her and returned home thanking the Lord. The Lord helped me by answering our prayers at both places. Bro. Alex and his wife invited me to their home. It was a Friday. Bro. Alex called his pastor and spoke to him on the phone in Spanish. I understood a little bit by his expression about what he was saying.

On the next day, Alex asked me to accompany him to his landlady's home. As he told her about these two miracles and about my stolen bag, that elderly woman prayed for us and gave me $300 and said, "Brother, you do not need to worry. Our God listens to our prayers, and He will meet our needs."

In the evening, Alex took me to his mother-in-law's home and told them about everything. She also prayed for me and put $250 in my hand saying, "The Lord bless you and help you, Pastor."

On Sunday morning, we went to Bro. Alex's church. The pastor gave me ten minutes to share my testimony after the praise and worship. After my testimony, the guest preacher gave the message. At the end, the church blessed me with $1,200. Now I had $1750. Hallelujah!

Satan robbed me of all that was in the bag, but I thank God He replaced the lost money with $50 more, a new passport, and a return air ticket. Our Lord slapped Satan's face. Praise the Lord (1 Thessalonians 5:16-18).

9

Formation of Living Hope Ministries

Anyone who wants to serve me must follow me, because my servants must be where I am. And the Father will honour anyone who serves me (John 12:26).

Until November 1986, my wife and I could not come to any agreement about moving to Delhi and serving there. Fixing our eyes on the Lord, we patiently waited for an answer from Him. I believe that, if the Lord does not speak to your spouse, one should not force it on her. We must wait for the Lord's time. If both are not of one mind, then how can they walk?

At the end of November 1986, my wife said, "In obedience to the Lord's call, we must go to that region which the Lord has shown you in a vision." Hearing this, I was joyful beyond limits. Then we started to pray with one mind. Finally on the evening of December 31, 1986, we committed ourselves to the Lord and waited for His timing.

The first week of January 1987 at Chennai, Tamilnadu during the India Every Home Crusade Leadership Conference, I submitted my resignation to the South Asia Director Bro. B.A.G. Prasad and requested his blessings to start a new work in the Northwest part of Delhi, where nearly two million people lived at that time. I had already surveyed that area. I found that a Baptist Church and a Brethren Assembly were the only churches in that area.

Formation of Living Hope Ministries

On May 3, 1987, being led by the Lord, we rented a house in Lok Vihar, Pitampura, Delhi. With the blessings of the EHC leadership, we moved our family there from Jaipur, Rajasthan, on the first day of June. The Lord showed me from His Word that to make myself accountable to anyone, I needed to establish a board. It was also necessary, because I knew that I could wander from the way and commit mistakes. The Word of God teaches us to give an account of all things (Hebrews 13:17; James 4:5), and that anyone serving the Lord is not self-sufficient or independent. The Lord revealed a name for the ministry from 1 Peter 1:3, "Living Hope" (Living Hope Ministries). I had personally visited some of the brethren and had shared the vision and urged them to pray. I wanted to be accountable to them. We took almost six months and then prayerfully proceeded to establish a society.

The names of the initial board members are: Chairman Dr. Enoch Anthony, Secretary; Rev. D.C. Kaushal, Treasurer; Bro. George Nyberg; Mr. Y. Samuel (Member); Mr. Gulshan Lal (Member); Mr. Masih Charan (Member); and Dr. J.O. Richard (Member). The ministry was registered on January 21, 1988. Today Living Hope has ministered in almost all of the states of north and north-west India.

Later on these friends of mine also served on the board of Living Hope Ministries from time to time: Dr. Victor Nazareth, Rev. V.S. Bhandari, Ps. Ezekiel Joshua, Ps. Dr. Josh Kallemal.

Our present board members are: Dr. Ps. Laji Paul, Chairman, Bro. Masih Charan, Vice Chairman, D.C. Kaushal, Secretary , Ps. Sam Banerjee, Treasurer, Dr. Gabriel Massey, Bro. Babykutty Ninan, Bro. Sunil Kumar, and Rev. Subodh John, Executive Director.

10

Ministry Expansion

For God is not unjust. He will not forget how hard you have worked for him and how you have shown your love to him by caring for other believers, as you still do (Hebrews 6:10).

At the beginning of the ministry in Delhi, I had turned fifty years of age and was ready for a new leap. We started with tract distribution during the day to every house in the slum areas and housing colonies in Pitampura, Rohini, and Rani Bagh, in northwest Delhi. If anyone asked for prayer, we prayed for the sick and others. We began to share the Gospel among the lepers in the Maleen slums of Shadipur Depot, near the Pusa Institute. This area had thousands of slum dwellers. Some families responded to the Gospel. If I wrote every single witness in this book, it would be beyond our capacity to print. Nevertheless, to encourage readers and for the glory of God, I will share briefly a few testimonies.

Badluram's Life Changed!

So you see, the Lord knows how to rescue godly people from their trials, even while keeping the wicked under punishment until the day of final judgment (2 Peter 2:9).

Badluram was a successful upper division clerk in the Haryana government in Chandigarh. He received a marriage

Ministry Expansion

proposal, which he accepted. Soon he was married. With a wife and two children, Badluram was a happy man.

A short time later his father-in-law, who had retired from the army, began to pressure Badluram to transfer all his property to his wife's name. But since Badluram's mother was alive, how could he do that? Widowed when Budluram was a child, his mother had raised him and his two sisters alone. He clearly refused his father-in-law. When his father-in-law saw that things were not working out his way, he took away his daughter along with the little children. He wanted to pressure Badluram. While leaving, he strictly warned that, if Badluram came to take his wife and children home, consequences would be bad. Furthermore, his father-in-law lodged a complaint against Badluram at the police station, saying that he was beating his wife and asking money from her father. So Badluram was sent to the district jail.

After a few years, Badluram was released from the prison. He had lost his mind and wandered here and there. He camped at Panipat's British Cemetery. While roaming about, he found and read our booklet, *New Life for You*, lying on the road. Seeing our address on the booklet, he found our house early one morning.

Hearing the doorbell, I opened the door and saw what seemed like a ghost standing in front of me. His beard and hair were overgrown and messy, and his clothes were torn and old. I asked him, "What do you want?"

"I want to meet D.C. Kaushal," he answered.

I replied reluctantly, "I am D.C. Kaushal. Please come in!"

I offered him tea, and then the first question he asked was, "Can your Jesus Christ deliver me? Can I have a new life?" He was alone and destitute with no relatives or friends. Poor Badluram was literally a victim of injustice, oppression, and loneliness.

I told him about the love of the Lord Jesus Christ and shared my testimony. I explained that, if you give your heart to the Lord Jesus and believe in Him, then all things are possible. "Your wife and your children will come back to you. Your life will be better. But you will have to believe that Jesus died on the cross for your sins, was buried, and rose again the third day. Lord Jesus is the only Saviour and Redeemer on earth. There is no one equal to Him. He loves you."

Badluram believed and repented of his sins and accepted the Lord Jesus. Then I prayed for him and sent him back.

A week later the bell rang at our house. It was Sunday morning. Expecting it to be the milkman, I opened the door. There stood a man dressed in clean clothes with a bag hanging on his shoulder, smiling at me. Before I could ask anything, he said, "I am Badluram! May I come in?"

"Who is Badluram?" I asked.

"I've come from Panipat!" he said. "A week ago, I came to you with the burden of my life. I had a Gospel booklet with me." His face reflected clear joy. I instantly remembered everything. I called him inside to sit and offered him breakfast. I was astonished to see the reflection of his joy. I hugged him. My wife and I shed tears of joy and praised the Lord. How wonderful is our Lord Jesus, "Emmanuel," God with us! The Lord Jesus is a Lifegiver. We exalt your name, Father, for your favours.

"Now I want to get baptised," he said. "I read the book you gave me and thought deeply on all the things. I have experienced true peace. Since that day, I sleep peacefully. I am very happy. I told my elderly mother about all this that happened. She said, 'Son, do what seems right to you! I am with you.'"

I baptised Badluram in the presence of three believers in the Prembadi canal of Pitampura. From there we went to church. During the worship, he testified of his new faith, of how Lord Jesus had delivered him from sins, curses, and wrongdoings, and had given him a new life full of joy and peace. "He transformed my life. Praise the Lord!"

We prayed for Badluram's wife and children to return. Soon after that, Badluram's wife was informed that her husband had been released from the prison, had come back home, and that his life had changed a lot. He was happier than before, free from all cares, and had dedicated his life to the Lord Jesus. Hearing this news, Badluram's wife returned with her children against the will of her father.

Badluram began sharing his testimony with more courage. All the statements in his testimony were convincing. He is the same Badluram, who in his madness would roam around in a shabby condition, but today Jesus changes lives, hears our prayer, and restores life. He delivers and fills us with joy and peace. Today Badluram is living joyfully with his family. His wife also received the Lord Jesus as her personal Lord and Saviour and was baptised in the same canal. Hallelujah!

Transformation of Ashok Kumar

Bro. Mahendra, who worked with the Delhi government, had accepted the Lord and was in fellowship with us. He shared his testimony with his elder Bro. Ashok, who worked for United India Insurance Company. Then Ashok accepted Jesus as his personal Lord and Saviour along with his family. Because of the testimony of these brothers, many people believed in the Lord Jesus, and the church began to grow. In those days, Satan also started to confuse, distract, and deceive new believers. As a result, some were enticed away by job offers and other material benefits offered by groups in their area. But the church continued to grow and seekers of truth came. There was peace and harmony among new growing believers. Teaching on discipleship continued. Meeting in houses were regular. Hallelujah!

Growth of the Church

By God's grace the work expanded in the states of Punjab, Delhi, and Orissa. To handle the task alone was difficult for me. Then Bro. Jeewan James came to us and, after serving with me for a while, we handed him the responsibility of the church in Delhi in April 1998. I could look after other matters.

Dayasagar Film

You didn't choose me. I chose you. I appointed you to go and produce lasting fruit, so that the Father will give you whatever you ask for, using my name (John 15:16).

In several villages of Haryana, Himachal Pradesh, and Punjab, we used the Dayasagar film, which made a very deep impact. People felt as if they were watching the Lord Jesus on film, seeing His love and power face to face. They believed in the Lord Jesus with open hearts and received the blessings of healing, peace, and deliverance. Ministering with the film was a unique experience for us. In short I would like to share how I got the opportunity to minister through the Dayasagar Film.

One day in October 1989 I received a phone call from the office of Dayspring International, Virginia Beach (USA). A woman asked me, "Is this D.C. Kaushal speaking?"

"Yes! Who are you? From where are you calling?" I replied.

"I am calling from Dayspring International office, USA. Our president, Dr. John Gilman, wants to meet you," she replied.

"Who is he?" I asked. "And why does he want to meet me?"

"I do not know. I was only asked to inform you. He is the president of the Dayspring International and is coming to Delhi by plane from Bombay. Please go to the Palam airport in Delhi to meet him."

"I do not know him, and I have never heard anything about him," I asked. "How will I recognise him and why should I meet him? I hope he is not an agent of any secret service."

She burst into loud laughter and said, "Brother, you are a man of great humour. He is just coming to meet you."

"When I don't know the purpose of meeting!" I said. "Neither have I known that person. Then why would I meet him at all? Why should I waste my time?"

The woman repeatedly requested, "Please make sure that you meet him once." She told me the time of his flight's arrival and the flight number.

I rode to the Palam Airport on my Lambretta scooter. As the woman had requested, I wrote "Dr. John Gilman" on a paper and waited for him. He came out of the airport and, seeing his name on the paper I held, he came to me and introduced himself. Then he said he wanted to go to my home. I was on a scooter, and he had a big suitcase besides a briefcase. It was difficult to carry all this on a scooter, and I hesitated to take a stranger to my house. Perceiving my dilemma, he said, "Brother, leave your scooter here in the parking lot. We will go by taxi."

Reaching my home, Dr. John Gillman introduced himself and told his purpose of coming to see us. "Who told you about me?" I asked.

"One of my friends who is yours too," he replied. "He told me about what you are doing and suggested that you are the right person for the work I have come here for." Then he asked me to share my testimony. He wanted to know my family, caste, religion, and why I accepted the Lord Jesus as my personal Saviour. I answered all his questions in detail.

"How will you accomplish this vision that God has given to you?" he asked.

I told him about presenting the good news through film

along with literature, Gospel meetings, street preaching, etc.

"How can a film share the Gospel?" he asked. Then I shared the experiences resulting from showing the film Dayasagar and Jesus.

He asked, "Which film do you use?"

"The Jesus Film and Dayasagar," I replied.

"What is the difference between these two?" he asked.

Villagers watching Dayasagar film

"The *Jesus Film* is based on the Gospel of Luke, but the *Dayasagar* script was written by a Catholic priest, and the film is for commercial purposes. There is dancing, drinking, singing, and even some scenes, which I do not like. But the last part of the *Dayasagar* film is very touching. Those who watch it feel that what is happening in front of their eyes are real. Therefore, most of those who see the film for the first time are in tears and shout, 'Why are you killing this innocent man? He has done nothing wrong. He fed the hungry, healed the sick, raised the dead, cleansed lepers, forgave the sinners! Why is such a person being crucified?' And some people with sticks and stones would shout, 'Stop! Stop! Do not kill him. Otherwise you will face the consequences. Such a view convicts us that this is the incarnation of God. He is not an ordinary person.'"

"Do you use this film?" he asked.

I told him that, while I served with Every Home Crusade, we used this, but now I did not have the film. I wanted to use it since it was a very effective tool for winning souls. He also asked how many people come to watch this film. I replied that, when we showed the film in a village, sometimes 150, 500, 1,000 people come to watch it.

He spent about five hours with me at the table. My wife, Sona, prepared simple food. Then he prayed and asked me to take him back to the airport. We took a taxi to the airport, and I returned home on my scooter. Sona asked who he was and why he came. I replied, "He is the owner of the *Dayasagar* film."

In February 1990, the same woman called me again. "Bro. Kaushal, how are you? I am calling from Dr. John Gilman's office."

I laughed and said, "Well, Dr. John Gilman who came to my house and did not even tell me where he came from and where he was going. Has he reached there?"

"He has returned. But now he is asking you to go to Amnapali in the last week of this month. I have been asked to inform you."

"Where is Amnapali?" I asked. "How do I reach there and why? Why is he calling me there? Sister, I don't have time to go there. What does he do there?"

"We have sent you a plane ticket. Soon you'll get it," she said. I was surprised that this person wanted me. I decided to go, wondering what he did there. But I did not know where Amnapali was. The air ticket arrived by mail, and it was from Delhi to Hyderabad. He had arranged someone to meet me at Hyderabad Airport and take me to his home to rest. Dr. John Gilman arranged for my travel by night train to Amnapali.

When I arrived at Amnapali Railway Station the next morning, Dr. John Gilman met me there joyfully. He asked me to give my testimony that evening at a convention in the open ground near a riverbank. The Komnapali brothers were ministering there. More than 5,000 people and some foreign preachers had also come. That evening I testified how God had saved and chosen me for His service 25 years earlier and how God had been blessing and using me for His service.

The next day I was asked to preach during the evening; and the third day, I was given the morning devotion. I was greatly blessed with their fellowship. About 150 people were baptised in the river. He asked me to stay for a day in Hyderabad where he had arranged my accommodation. When Dr. Gilman arrived in Hyderabad, we had the opportunity to learn more about each other. Once again, I asked him who had told him about me. Simply he told me, "Brother, I promised him I would not tell you his name. He is your friend and mine too. I cannot break my word at any cost."

It was time for me to return to Delhi, so I thanked him and said goodbye. When I was about to leave, he put a heavy envelope in my hand and asked me to open it only after reaching home. I was delighted, thinking Dr. Gilman must have filled this envelope with a lot of Indian money. I reached home thanking the Lord.

"How was the trip?" Sona asked.

"Very good," I replied.

Then I took out the envelope and showed it to my wife saying, "Dr. Gilman has given this." We eagerly opened the envelope, expecting a large stack of Indian money in it. But after opening it, we both laughed loud. There were only papers inside the envelope. It had the *Dayasagar* film's papers, saying that the film script, generator, and projector etc. worth 60,000 Indian rupee were sent through air cargo from Hyderabad to Delhi.

I was surprised and was very grateful to the Lord for this miracle. The Lord meets the needs of His people in amazing ways. We meet people who say that, through the *Dayasagar* film, they have come to know the Lord Jesus as their personal Lord and Saviour.

Ministry Expansion

I know that the *Dayasagar* film has been successful in touching thousands of lives. It has also contributed in showing the way of salvation to people. We showed the film in 128 villages in the state of Punjab, and thus, many believed in the Lord and accepted him as their personal Lord and Saviour. Many received complete healing, some were delivered from demonic spirits, and others received the Lord Jesus. Three people had died, but the Lord raised them back to life. Many family problems were solved. Some families who had no children for 10, 12, 15 years, had spent their money but with no result were blessed with children. In 72 villages, we established small fellowships through the film ministry. Yet I believe that complete figures will be known only when we reach heaven. I still support broadcasting the word of God through media.

11

Adult Literacy Programme

Hundreds of people came to the Lord through the *Dayasagar* film, most of whom were completely illiterate. Though I enjoyed listening to their testimonies, I felt burdened about how I could help them grow in their new faith. Then the Lord put in my heart that I should start an adult literacy program. Learning to read and write would help them understand the Word of God and edify them. I tried to contact a few organisations in India who are involved in adult literacy but got no response.

In January 2002, we had a guest from Australia at our house. After a long conversation before leaving, he asked me about our number one need so they could pray. I told him about my need to arrange adult literacy classes for our new believers in the Punjab and other states. Then he prayed and left. On March 21, 2002 at 3:45 a.m., I received a phone call.

"Are you D.C. Kaushal?"

"Yes!" I said.

"I am Eric Leach, calling from Australia," he said. "I have good news for you. You want to educate new believers who are illiterate to read and write. I shared this matter about you with my prayer group. We would like to help you with this need." He asked me to give him the statistics of those villages' financial, political, and religious conditions, and where I wanted to run the adult literacy class. He asked how I would work on this pro-

Adult Literacy Programme

ject. I asked for two weeks' time and engaged a Christian brother who had retired from his work with the Punjab Government Education Department. After two weeks, I sent a report to Bro. Eric Leach. He provided funds for the project and checked its account in person.

At first, adult literacy centres were opened in Punjab. Hundreds of people who had come to faith came to these literacy centres for classes. People from Rajasthan, Western-UP, Himachal Pradesh, and Haryana also benefitted from these literacy centres.

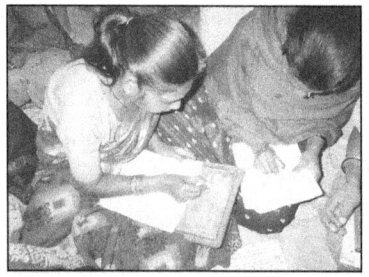

Literacy class, Gumtala Village

Certificate distribution

A Testimony of Mrs. Chinder

Adult literacy classes were organised for three months in Gumtala village near Amritsar City (Punjab). A family with two children lived there. The wife, Chinder, was illiterate. Since her childhood, she always wished to study. One day during her childhood, while watching her neighbour's child going to school in a school dress, she said to her father, "Papa, I want to go to school."

Her father angrily slapped her so hard on her left ear that the other ear started bleeding. Her father yelled at her said, "We never studied, so now you will go to school!"

Many years have passed since the incident. Today Chinder is a married woman and the mother of two children. When she found out that adult literacy classes were going to start in her neighbourhood, she asked her husband, "Shall I go there to study?"

"If you have time, then go for it," he answered. Chinder started coming to our adult literacy classes and completed the three-month course.

Graduation day came and we asked those who came to study to share their experience. Some described their experiences about how they can now read and write. "We can read our Bible," they replied.

We asked Sister Chinder, "Would you like to share?" On hearing this, she began to sob and couldn't stop. With much difficulty, we calmed her down. Then she narrated her life's story from her father's negative response during childhood to her husband's positive response in coming for the adult education. She said, "Now I can read as well as write. I can write my name; I can read the bus number; I can write letters too. I have started reading my Bible."

We thanked the Lord Jesus for her happiness. We expressed our heartfelt gratitude to the donors who gave 500 Punjabi Bibles, to Bro. Eric for providing the necessary funds, and to Mr. Adarsh Maxton and Bro. Prakash Masih for coordinating the adult literacy project.

Even today most of the women in our country are not educated, and those who wish to study are crushed in their childhood days. We must pray that every family can educate and save their girls, not discriminating between boys and girls. Amen!

Adult Literacy Programme

My Life Changed by Dharampal

This means that anyone who belongs to Christ has become a new person. The old life is gone; a new life has begun! (2 Corinthians 5:17)

The following is the firsthand story of Dharampal:

The Prince of Peace changed my life. Before accepting the Lord Jesus, I went to temples and gurdwaras, but I never went to church. I had started smoking and drinking with my friends. Later I started living in the ashrams with sadhus and served them. There I also started taking bhang as a narcotic. I was there for about ten years with them. One day my two older sisters came to take me home.

The Sadhu, the main guru with whom I lived, said, "Dharampal, your sisters have come to take you home. They will surely get you married. Do not marry because our master guru curses men who marry after becoming his disciple. And he would never have a son."

My sisters asked me to go home, and I went with them. I started working in a factory. My sisters arranged my marriage. The next year, my wife gave birth to a boy, but he was born dead. After that another son came, but the same thing happened to him. I thought maybe having a child was not in my fate.

Meanwhile, my wife believed in the Lord Jesus Christ, confessed her sins, accepted Jesus as her personal Lord and Saviour, and took immersion baptism. After that a healthy girl was born in April 1997. At the same time, my thoughts lingered on that sadhu's words that I should not get married:"You will never have a son." I thought his words turned out to be true because my two sons were born dead but the girl was born healthy.

"Since I have accepted the Lord Jesus, we have found so much peace, and God has blessed us with a baby girl as a gift," said my wife daily. "You should also start coming to church with me and confess the Lord Jesus. He will comfort you. You always are sick. He will heal you and give us a son."

"If you want to go to church, you go," I replied. "But I will not go. I don't want to become a Christian."

Then my wife began praying and fasting for me. After about six months, I went to church one Sunday to please my wife. There I heard from the Holy Bible about the forgiveness of sins in Jesus. Thereafter I started going to church regularly. Then I found out that I was born in sin and I am a sinner. Because of my sins, I am very miserable and I need the Lord Jesus. In March 1998, I repented of my sins and accepted the Lord Jesus as my Saviour, and was baptised. The Lord Jesus transformed my life.

Again, the hope of having a child arose in our family. I prayed, "Lord Jesus, children are a gift from you. If you can give a son to Abraham in his old age, then why not me?" Before the birth of my child, by faith I named him Isaac and, by the grace of God, on December 5, 2000, God blessed us with a son. I was thankful to the Lord God, and my faith in the Lord was strengthened. I said to the Lord, "The Sadhu had said that my family will never have a son, but Lord You proved his words wrong and gave me a son according to Your Word."

I grew in faith in the Lord and the Word of God. I had a desire to study God's Word in Bible College and through Bro. Hira Masih I came in contact with Pastor D.C. Kaushal. The Lord opened the way to study in his Bible school in Gurgaon, Haryana. Now I have been serving with the Living Hope Ministry ever since. I thank the Lord that He gave me physical healing and blessed me with a daughter and a son. And the best thing is that He is using me as a witness for His love and name. So far, 130 people have accepted Christ as their Saviour in our church, out of which 98 people obeyed in baptism and testified. From the depths of my heart I really thank the Lord. All honour and glory be to our Lord Jesus Christ! Hallelujah!

And the Child Came Back to Life

I tell you the truth, anyone who believes in me will do the same works I have done, and even greater works, because I am going to be with the Father (John 14:12).

Bhago had a son and a daughter. Her husband was a truck driver. Due to his work as a truck driver, her husband often had to stay away from home for a long time. So, during that time, she had to take care of herself and her children alone. They belong to Jatt Sikh.

A preacher named Balwinder John came once a week to her neighbour's house and shared the word of God there. Well, it was all a very normal thing for them, but we know that when the Lord is at work in someone's life, it happens in His time (John 15:16). This house had a courtyard, with enough space for people to sit in.

One day, Balwinder John came and began to tell people about the miracle that Jesus did for Lazarus. Doing chores in her courtyard, Bhago listened to the preacher's words attentively. The preacher told of how Lazarus had died and had been buried four days. The Lord Jesus had said to his family, "If you believe, then you will see the work of God." (John 11:25-

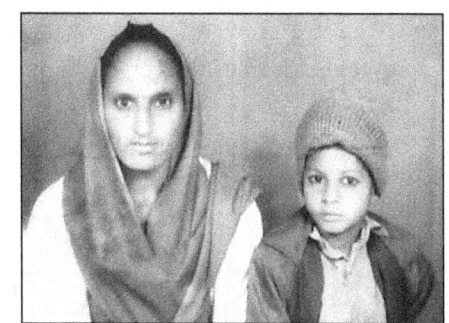

Sister Bhaago with her son

26). Jesus asked them, where they had put him. And the family took Jesus to the grave of Lazarus. On reaching the grave of Lazarus, Jesus cried out with a loud voice, "O Lazarus, come out!" (John 11:43). The people said that there must be a stench by now. Lazarus, wrapped in linen, came out and stood before them. God raised a four days' dead man alive, and the people thanked God (John 11:44). The preacher explained the power of the Lord by these words. Bhago heard all this.

After some time, Bhago's son became so sick that he had to be taken to the hospital. But her husband was at work, so Bhago decided to take her son to the hospital in the city. She waited for transportation on the road. After a while an auto rickshaw came and she requested, "Please take me to the city hospital; my son is very sick." The auto rickshaw driver took them to drop them at the hospital. About five kilometres from the hospital, his rickshaw's tire went flat. Then she had to ask for assistance from a bike rider. The bike rider took her to the hospital. Upon reaching the hospital, the doctor checked the child and found that he was dead. He immediately began to shout at Bhago, saying, "What wrong have I done to you? Why have you brought the dead child here? It's too late. He is already dead."

After hearing this, she became numb. When she had left her home, the child was alive. She begged the doctor, "Please check him again, Doctor Sahab! I brought him alive. How can that be?"

But the doctor yelled again, demanding her to take her son and leave immediately. "The child is dead." The doctor called the nurse and a security guard to get Bhago out.

Then she started weeping and slowly a crowd began to gather around her. Everybody told her that her child was dead. "Take him home."

Bhago wept bitterly. Then someone in the crowd called out,

"Cry out to your God! Maybe He will listen to you!" At that she remembered what the preacher had said about how Lazarus had been dead for four days when Jesus called his name. Sitting near the dead body of her child, she began to pray with tears in her eyes. Ignoring the voices of those around her, she continued asking Jesus. A half an hour later, the boy suddenly opened his eyes and, seeing the people around, was startled. When the doctors heard this, they came out. Stunned by what they saw, they asked Bhago what had happened.

"One day a Christian preacher came to our neighbouring house and preached about how Lord Jesus had raised a man after four days of being dead," she answered. "I also prayed to Jesus Christ, and He heard my cry and gave life back to my son. See, he is alive!"

Everyone was amazed by this miracle and the name of the Lord Jesus was glorified. In Mark 9:23 it is written, "Jesus said to him, 'If you can believe, all things are possible to him who believes.'"

Even today, Sister Bhago testifies about this miracle of the Lord Jesus from village to village and shares the Gospel about the Lord Jesus with people. Hallelujah!

12

Cried Seeing the Poverty

A young man, Samuel Das, from Orissa State came to us in July 1988. After three months with us, he told us that he wanted to go to his people and stay with them to share the Gospel among them. He went back and ministered among his region in the Dharamgarh area where people understood Hindi very well. It was about 15 kilometers away from Madhya Pradesh border. Bro. Samuel Das called me to visit him. When I went to meet the people, I saw how they lived in pathetic poverty. The men and women who lived there covered only half of their bodies. Children between the ages of 10-12 wandered around, naked and hungry. Seeing the famine, starvation, and poverty shook me. Famine was severe in this northwest part of Orissa where there had been no rain for the past three years. Our central government at that time was also concerned for that region.

Later I understood that it was the Lord's plan that I see all this. I returned home with a heavy heart, strongly feeling that the Lord wanted me to do something for the children there. I shared the matter with our church and the board of Living Hope Ministries. We began to pray, "Lord, show us the way to save those children's futures from destruction."

Children's Home at Dharamgarh, Odissha

During my visit, the Lord led me in their midst to start a

ministry for children and to release people from the powers of darkness by proclaiming the Word of God.

In July 1990, we started the ministry with 39 children in Dharamgarh, Orissa, in a house we rented. Our church in Rohini, New Delhi, gave special offerings for the basic needs of the children like clothes, books, and other needs. Only the rent of the house was borne by Living Hope.

This children's home ministry was at first taken care of by Bro. Samuel Das. After a while we sent Bro. Samuel and his wife to Bible school for church planting courses. This ministry moved smoothly. So Bro. David Raut and his family came to look after the children and taught them good discipline and enhanced their spiritual level. I am very grateful to him and his family for their contribution. These testimonies still help me to be courageous in every situation.

God Who Meets Our Needs

In April 1992 the building work of the children's home in Dharamgarh began. We believed that God would provide for everything. We purchased a half acre of land about three kilometres from Dharamgarh on the canal side of Sinapali and began the construction work. First, we dug a well because there was no source of water. Pastor Wilfred Paul of Masihi Mandali (the Believers Fellowship) in Dehradun, ministered in England among Asians in the Bolton City.

Meanwhile, on one Monday evening, I received a phone call from Bro. David Bullock of England. He told me

that he wanted to send money for the children's home in Orissa. I told him that he could write a bank draft in the name of Living Hope Ministries and send it under registered post.

After that I visited Dharamgarh and convinced the contractor that we would get his money as soon as possible. "Have faith in us," I pled. I was in Dharamgarh for a week with no facility to make a trunk call. I had to travel 50 kilometres from there to Bhawanipatna. I called our accountant Bro. Abraham Varghese at Delhi office and asked, "Have we received any money?"

"Yes, from England, a person named David Bullock has sent a bank draft of Rs. 26,750/=," answered Bro. Abraham.

After hearing this, I cried tears of joy. I cannot describe how thankful I was to the Lord. "Send this money immediately to Dharamgarh Branch Account," I said to Abraham. We had already opened an account in the State Bank of India, Dharamgarh, Orissa.

I told the contractor that he would receive his money in 3-4 days. I did not know David Bullock, but he sent money to us at a time when we needed it desperately. The Lord is truly our provider. Hallelujah!

Meeting Dave Bullock

The following is Dave Bullock writing about our meeting together in his own words.

One Sunday morning in June 1994 I woke up crying. My heart felt broken, but I didn't know why; and even my wife Jean couldn't console me. Later, God revealed the reason during the morning service at Bolton Pentecostal Church. It was for "the children" but which children? Then He instructed me to stand on the platform and ask the church to help these children.

People shouted out, "Who are these children? How can we help?"

Cried Seeing the Poverty

I continued crying, "These are the Lord's tears," I exclaimed because I still didn't know myself. But the congregation agreed to help anyway. Praise the Lord!

Later on God informed me that we were to raise money, but He didn't say for whom. This was a real test of faith and obedience, and the church responded faithfully. That October we collected all kinds of good quality clothing and other salable items, and held a second-hand sale in front of the Bolton Town Hall, from which we raised £500. (We were truly blessed!) But we still didn't know what to do with this money and so placed it in the church mission fund, awaiting God's instructions. Six months went by until one Sunday morning in May 1995 when I was at the church. Someone had given me two leaflets of potential missions to pray over, Siloam Ministries and Living Hope Ministries. I knew the first one but hadn't heard of the other. Then while I was praying, the main doors opened and through them walked an Asian gentleman whom I'd never spoken to before—Bro. Wilfred Paul. I asked for his advice. He explained that he was a very close friend of Living Hope's founder, D.C. Kaushal, and that this was where he felt the money should go since they were building an orphanage in the state of Orissa for destitute children.

That June we sent a bank draft for 25,750 Rupees off to India, and later received a receipt for it by return of post. Sadly, just a short time after, Wilfred Paul went to be with the Lord, and I felt compelled to attend his funeral service. To my surprise, the guest speaker was D.C. Kaushal. I made sure that we met afterwards. This was when Jean and I learned of the miracle. D.C. and his wife Sona explained how they had been promised money to have a well dug at the orphanage in Dharamgarh. The money never came, and death threats were made against manager, David Rout, and D.C. if the contractor wasn't paid. Then the deadline for payment came! D.C. had assembled the children for a night of prayer, believing that God would supply their needs. The next morning David Rout took D.C. to the S.T.D. phone to ask Sona if the money had arrived. She replied that it hadn't, but that there was an envelope from England marked "Personal" that she hadn't opened. D.C. asked her to open it. And when she did, she found our bank draft inside. D.C asked Sona to give the draft to Bro. Abraham Varghese, Accountant.

Can you believe it? It was for the exact amount needed to pay the contractor, and yet God had planned for this a *year before* it was needed, and, on the other side of the world! This is our God! Hallelujah! And this was also the beginning of a God-made friendship that is still alive today. It was also the birthing for numerous missionary visits to India, and a love affair with a nation whom I have grown to love more with every visit. During successive visits to India, we have experienced God's miraculous power, His unfailing love, and His saving grace over and over again, the likes of which I haven't witnessed here in England.

Some of Those Miracles

Dave continues:

In Babehalli village we witnessed a young girl with a really bad stutter begin to speak clearly after receiving prayer. A baby was healed of pneumonia, and several people of malaria in Gumtala Colony, near Amritsar city. Then there was the young, married couple in Atari Village, who'd been told by doctors that they couldn't have any children. We prayed with them, and a year later D.C. joyfully told me of the arrival of their first baby.

These miracles in Punjab were one aspect of God's love, and we experienced another in Orissa. Watching the orphanage being built over the next couple of years, and seeing the children develop life skills, with many coming to a faith in Jesus, has been a real blessing to us. Some children have done so well that they were funded to go on to college. Absolutely amazing!

But even our visits to Dharamgarh didn't go without us seeing miracles. During our first visit while travelling by car through the jungle, I was attacked by what later turned out to be Afro Indian crossed, killer bees. Soon my chest was tightening and I began to lose consciousness. Our driver was rushing me to a nearby leprosy hospital when we remembered prayer! D.C., Sona, and Jean laid hands on me and were amazed as my pain eased and the lumps from the stings began to disappear.

My next visit to India was no less spectacular. D.C. once again took me to Punjab. During one service we prayed for a little girl who had never been able to speak from birth. What a blessing, the first word on her lips was "Yesu" (Jesus). Then, sadly we were summoned to a hospital in Amritsar where Pastor Hira's wife lay seriously ill from having yet again miscarriage. We prayed that God would heal her and give them a child. A year later they had a healthy baby boy. Praise the Lord!

Definitely the greatest of God's miracles, other than salvation, that I have ever been privileged to be part of must be when I'd preached in one of the border villages. We made the usual appeal to those needing prayer, when a group of woman who had been wailing throughout the service came forward, together with their friend who was covered by a large blanket. They pulled the blanket away to reveal eight year old Jitu being held in her mother's arms. The girl's legs and arms hung limply, her eyes stared into space, and nothing moved. I thought that D.C. said that she was dying of polio, and so I laid hands on her head, prayed, "In the name of Jesus," and immediately the girl cried out. Everyone was jumping and shouting with joy. It was a year later that I discovered what had actually happened. The girl had been dead! She is now married, and many in her village have turned to Jesus as their Saviour.

Then, on another visit to India, we visited Roriwal Village where fifteen-year-old Rani lived. She suffered with severe asthma, and we were called to pray with her as she had become unconscious. She was healed immediately and stood up. She is now married to Prem Masih. They have a son and attend their local church.

On another occasion we visited Gumtala Colony where we were asked by Lovepreet's parents to pray for him. He was unconscious from an incurable brain disease. The doctors gave him no hope. We laid hands on the five year old, and God instantly healed him! Praise the Lord!

Then there was the time when Paul Crossley and I were holding a training session for pastors and their wives at Gumtala. A Sikh family wandered in and sat down to listen. I preached the Gospel instead. I couldn't take my eyes off their son, Kuldeep Singh. Right from birth, he couldn't communicate at all, never smiled, and spun around as he shuffled to walk. During a break, D.C. introduced me to the mother and father. They wanted us to pray for their son. God prompted me to first challenge them about Jesus as Saviour. They committed their lives to Him and so we all laid hands on Kuldeep and prayed for healing. Then they left. The following morning they arrived, together with their other son who was talking to Kuldeep. But now Kuldeep was walking in a straight line, laughing, and trying to answer his brother. He was healed, and his parents saved. Hallelujah!

I could go on and on about wonderful India and our awesome, amazing God, but space doesn't permit. Suffice it to say that out of a single, miraculous meeting with Wilfred Paul, Jean and I were privileged to meet and become close friends with D.C. Kaushal and his family, which includes "Living Hope Ministries." And because of this, we witnessed so many amazing miracles in the name of Jesus, all of which have served to grow and build up our faith in His name. Thank You, Lord, and thank you, India!

After awhile the roof of the children's home building was about to be constructed, but we could not afford to buy cement and iron bars. So we stopped the work for a while. We did not want to borrow because we put ourselves into a form of slavery when we borrow. I learned to trust in the Lord from the Word of God. We prayed for our needs, trusting the Lord's promises.

Meanwhile I received a letter from the USA. The person who wrote asked some strange questions like, "Should women wear a head covering in the church?" and "Should they have a pastoral ministry?" and "Should a little differences lead to a divorce?" and "Should women be teachers in churches?" and so on. I did not know that person, but answering his questions in the letter, I asked, "Brother, who are you? Give me full information about yourself; and how do you know about me?" After some weeks his second letter came. He shared his complete information and wrote that he was satisfied with all my answers.

He further wrote, "I am the only son of my parents. Since my marriage, I am living away from them. Not long ago, one after another, my parents went to be with the Lord. They had a petrol pump and owned house. One night my wife with my 5-year-old son suddenly left home without telling me. It has been 17 years now. I am still waiting for my wife and son to return. I do not even close the door of my house at night because I think that one day they will return. I have forgiven my wife and will accept her. My heart and doors of my home are open for her. You pray for me that soon I might be able to have my son and my wife at home."

He also wrote, "I have a friend who is also your friend and he told me about your life and ministry. After his parents died, he sold all their possessions and sent the money to different institutions. I do not lack money. I have a job and the Lord meets all my needs. I am sending this small gift for your ministry. You can use this offering however you like. I do not need your response to this letter nor do I need photos of how you spent the money. I am satisfied with your friend's testimony. I am praying for you. God, bless you!"

Our God is so good! God's Word says, "Even before you ask Me, I have heard you" (Isaiah 26: 3-4). I gave that check to my accountant, Abraham saying, "This is a $1,000 check. Deposit it in the bank."

When Abraham saw that check, he said in amazement, "Uncle, it is a $10,000 check! Look at it carefully." I could not believe what I saw. It was a $10,000 check! We thanked the Lord again and again. Our God never fails. Hallelujah!

How wonderfully He fulfils our needs! The money that we received helped complete the roof of the children's home. The construction work was now finished, and we dedicated the building. Bro. David Raut's family and all the children moved into the Children's Home. What a blessing. All honour and praise to the Lord.

Meeting God's Servant

In November 1990 there was a World Charismatic Conference in Atlanta, GA, USA. Rev. Bhandari's friend from Florida, USA, was with him but due to continual rain, he could not arrange any gospel meetings. So he called me and asked if I could arrange a meeting for his pastor friends in Delhi so I did arranged the meeting. The pastor was a very typical charismatic but we had a very fruitful meeting in Rohini area in Delhi.

Cried Seeing the Poverty

Several people were healed and some had accepted the Lord Jesus as their personal Lord and Savior. Praise the Lord!

On his return to USA he sent me information on the World Charismatic Conference in Atlanta, GA, USA, and urged me to attend it. I asked him several questions about the conference. After much thinking and prayers, I wrote to the conference coordinator. I was satisfied with his response to my enquiry, and he sent me the invitation letter saying they would provide free accommodation and my round trip air ticket. I was happy. The conference was in November 1990. There were several top leaders like Dr. Oral Roberts and others. My stay was arranged with a black young family (Afro-American). On the second day before lunch break, the conference coordinator announced that they had paid all the foreign participants' airfares both ways, and their stay had been arranged with church families. Then some foreign delegates came out of the meeting, and I also came out as we were not paid. In the church foyer was a book display by Pastor Don Nori of Destiny Image Publishers. I started looking at his display after a while, and he asked me why I was not attending the conference. I explained the reason. He was very disturbed.

Dr. Bertist Rouse

I contacted Dr. Jack McAllister's friend Bro. Garret Gustafson in Mobile, Alabama. He came the next day to meet me and after hearing he asked me to spend some time with his family in Mobile. Then he introduced me to Dr. Bertist Rouse, President of International Gospel Outreach, a very humble soul and full of passion for people without Christ. This was during the Thanksgiving celebration in November in the USA. Later he visited us in Orissa, Delhi, and Amritsar, Punjab, on his way to Pakistan in March 1995. Healthwise he was not very strong. His son Tom Rouse and his friend Bro. Doug Philip from Trinity Church in Jonesboro, Arkansas, accompanied him. We went to Dharamgarh Children's Home and had meetings in the Sinnapali area of Dharamgarh Tehsil. Many people accepted the Lord as their personal Savior and some were baptised in the Mahananda River in the Sinnapali area. We arranged their stay at the PWD guest house at Dhramgarh. It was a very painful experience for him but he never complained. He was all the time in a happy mood, encouraging the pastors of Living Hope in that area. It was a very learning experience as the Lord's servant, in spite of his weak health and culture shock, never complained. He spoke to us like Nehemiah of the Old Testament.

When he reached Pakistan a few days later, I received a phone call from his office in USA saying he was very sick and admitted to the hospital at Islamabad in Pakistan. He needed our prayers. Thank God by His grace after two weeks in the hospital, he flew back to the US safely. "Our God is a good God. He cares for his chosen servants" (Jeremiah 17:14). Hallelujah!

A few years later, Bro. Raut's family had to move to Bhubaneswar City due to their children's education. His eldest daughter wanted to study medical science. After they left, we were unable to find anyone dedicated to serving the children. After much prayer and thinking about what would be best for the children's future, the board of LHM decided to hand over this ministry to an organisation that was already into children's ministry.

In 2002, the board handed Bal-Ashram children's home to the Indian Missionary Society of Chennai. Many children who were educated there are well settled now. Some are preachers, some own businesses, and some are teachers. Some girls are nurses, and some are married now and leading their families. To God be the glory! Today about 75 children are being educated there. I want to thank specifically Bro. Dave and Jean Bullock, Bolton Pentecostal Church, Bro. Alex Rivera and his wife Laurie, Bob Newsteadt, my friend Dr. Burtis Rouse, and other prayer partners for their financial help and prayers.

Meeting Bill Barr and His Mother

In October 1994, due to some urgent work, I went to Main Market, Connaught Place, in New Delhi, with my wife, Sona, daughter, Vinita, and son Sunil. When turning from Connaught Circus to Janpath, we saw two foreigners coming our direction. My son Sunil said to me, "Daddy, look who's coming!" I saw a white-haired woman and man coming toward us.

Bill Barr

Seeing the clothes and full beard of the man, my daughter Vinita asked with curiosity, "Daddy, ask this person where he is from."

I said, "Okay! Let him come closer."

As they came closer, my daughter insisted, "Daddy, ask him!"

I don't know why, but I perceived that he was a Christian. When they came very close to us, again my daughter said, "Daddy, please ask!"

I laughed and at last, I said, "Hello Brother! Are you a Christian?"

He immediately answered, "Yes! Praise the Lord!"

Wow! In confusion I asked, "From where?"

"America," he said.

"What is your name?" I asked.

"Bill Barr," he said.

"Oh! Wow!" With great surprise I said, "Are you the son of Missionary William D. Barr in Khanna Mandi, Punjab?"

He jumped and said, "Oh yes! Yes! I am his son, and this is my mother." He said pointing at the older woman.

I spoke to his mother and said, "Sister, I once stayed in your home in September 1965. At that time, I was working with the Bible Society of India, New Delhi."

She instantly recognised me, "Oh! Are you D.C. Kaushal?"

"Yes! I am." I said. Thus, she was pleased to meet me and my family on the road. After this we had tea together and interacted. Later they visited us in Pitampura, West Delhi.

Bro. Bill came to India frequently to teach at Youth with a Mission bases and to serve other places. On my request, he later came to Punjab. At that time, we were running a Bible school in Amritsar, Punjab, where the majority of students were Punjabi. Bill had a good knowledge of the Punjabi language and Sikhism.

Bible School Shifted to Gurgaon

Bro. Vachan Singh Bhandari's friend, Bro. Ingemar, helped us while staying in Amritsar in 1997. Because he was a Swedish missionary's son, Ingemar's Hindi was good. He was born in the Chandrubar area of Maharashtra State and received his high school education in India. He had good experience in serving with an Operation Mobilization team.

On March 21, 1998, we bought a plot in Gurgaon for the Bible school. In the month of September of the same year, the construction work began. Not wanting to disrupt our work, we rented a house in Gurgaon and started our Bible school there.

A young man named Chris Dickerson came to us from the

USA. My good friend Dr. Burtist Rouse, president of International Gospel Outreach, had recommended that he come to us for practical experience as he had already completed his Bible course. Bro. Ingemar had come from Sweden to help us in teaching for nine months. He was already in Faridabad, helping other short term study programs.

My dear Bro. Bill came for two weeks to teach at the Bible School at my invitation. On January 25, 1999 we spent the whole night in prayer and preparation to distribute gospel tracts on the next day, our Republic Day, and to watch the parade at Rajpath, India Gate, in New Delhi. So we gave the responsibilities to Bro. Chris for the Connaught Place side (North) and Sufdarjung Hospital side (South) to Bro. Ingemar.

The Road Accident

While leaving early morning for New Delhi to watch the parade and distribute gospel tracts, Bro. Bill Barr said he would go with Bro. Ingemar on the motorcycle, not in the jeep with Bro. Chris and students.

"You don't have a helmet," I said.

"Don't worry, Brother," he replied. "I will put on my turban."

I tried to help him understand that he was a foreigner and a Christian, not Sardar Ji (a Sikh man), but he did not listen to my advice. Finally, after prayers everyone left for India Gate, New Delhi. I remained at the training Center because no one else was there. Bro. Ingemar and Bro. Bill Barr were on the motorcycle behind the jeep. As soon as the motorcycle turned towards New Delhi on the main road, there was a speed breaker on the road. Suddenly a stray dog ran in front.

While applying brakes to save the dog, Ingemar lost his balance, and the motorcycle bounced off the speed breaker. Everything happened so suddenly that no one knows exactly what occurred. Both men were thrown off headlong. Ingemar sustained less injury since he was wearing a helmet; but while soaring, Bill's turban had fallen off and his head hit hard on the ground. It was very shocking. He immediately became unconscious. His mouth, nose, and ears were bleeding. The brothers in the jeep screamed after seeing them fall and stopped the jeep. People gathered around quickly to help. Bro. Chris called me on the phone.

I arrived at the scene without losing any time and was shocked to see their plight. We immediately rushed them to the Saraswati Hospital in Gurgaon. After seeing their condition, the doctor told us, "We can help one (Ingemar), but we can't do anything for the other (Bill). We don't have many facilities. Take him to Delhi to AIIMS Hospital as soon as possible."

We called AIIMS and were told that, because it was a national public holiday, doctors were not available in the trauma centers. The junior doctors on duty were not able to handle this. Then I contacted Sister Biro Samuel who got Bill admitted to a trauma centre in Malviya Nagar, New Delhi.

I made every effort to hide my tears. I was totally confused. What will I say to Bro. Bill's wife and his mother? Will they forgive me? How will I comfort his daughter and wife when they arrive back in New Delhi? What should I do? From Gurgaon Hospital to the trauma center in Malviya Nagar, these thoughts blinded me like snow. I could not understand anything. I wanted to cry but couldn't. Due to the serious head injury, Bro. Bill was in a coma.

We reported the entire incident to his family immediately and told them to come as soon as they could. After three days, Sister Cheryl and their daughter Jody arrived in India.

To care for Bill, a person needed to be with him all the time. Chris, Basant Lama, Bible School students, and I stayed with

Cried Seeing the Poverty

him one by one, day and night. We prayed constantly for his recovery and well-being. We had a prayer chain. What else could we do in such a situation except pray and call on our loving God for help? We had no other way. We had never faced such a tragedy. There is no better medicine than prayer and no greater physician than the Lord Jesus.

When his wife and daughter arrived in Delhi, they were shocked to see Bill's condition. But all glory be to God, they gathered themselves and, seeing this challenging situation, they stood firm in faith and continually asked for help from the Lord in prayers.

I look up to the mountains—does my help come from there? My help comes from the Lord, who made heaven and earth! (Psalm 121:1-2)

Jesus told her, "I am the resurrection and the life. Anyone who believes in me will live, even after dying" (John 11:25).

Sister Cheryl urged the doctors to help them take Bill back home to the USA. Was it possible in this condition? Meanwhile, Bill's brother, Don Barr, had also come from the Philippines. Cheryl and Jody were greatly strengthened by his presence. Now they had a man from their family.

Three weeks after the accident, Bill's condition was more stable though he was still in a coma in the hospital. Doctors and friends in India and in the USA helped make arrangements to fly him home. An Indian doctor and nurse travelled with him to provide care the entire way. After reaching there, he was admitted to a hospital. He gradually gained consciousness but was very confused. Sister Cheryl regularly updated me about Bill's condition. His recovery was slow. The same year in May 1999, it came in my mind to visit Bro. Bill Barr. I expressed my desire to see Bill by going to America. With great affection, Sister Cheryl invited me to come.

The moment Sister Cheryl and I entered Bro. Bill's hospital room and were a little distance from his bed, Bill suddenly said in Punjabi language,"Oh Paaji! Tussi aa Gaye?" ("Brother Ji, you have come.") Cheerfully he began to talk to me. "Oh, my Lord! Thank you!" Bro. Bill was out of a coma by then, but he was still in a state of confusion. As Bro. Bill talked to me, his family stood amazed as he asked about my work and family in India. Listening to this, they praised the Lord. Nobody had expected such a change in his condition. It was a miracle of God. Hallelujah!

I was with Bill for three days during which he asked me about all the details of the road accident in Gurgaon. How did the accident happen? What happened after that? How was he treated? What places was he taken to? How was his condition? He asked me everything in detail, and his wife and daughter were surprised. I told him all the things of that day.

He recovered quickly thereafter and, three years later, he came again to India with his wife. They went to all the places here: where the accident took place, the Saraswati Hospital where he was taken at first, and then to the trauma hospital in New Delhi where he was admitted for three weeks. Together we rejoiced that the Lord Jesus used so many people and saved his life.

Then they went back to the USA. Even today he is still influenced by the incident. He is very thankful for how the Lord saved him that day from the fatal accident and how the Lord brought him out of a coma. In all these things, the Lord be glorified. "The righteous person faces many troubles, but the Lord comes to the rescue each time" (Psalm 34:19). Hallelujah!

13

Mercy Children's Home, Amritsar

In order to begin the ministry of Bal-Ashram at a local level in 2005, we bought about four acres of land in the village of Dhulawat in the district of Gurgaon, Haryana. We started the construction work. The boundary wall was complete and the preparation to lay the foundation of the children's home was ready. One day I was visiting the Bible Society Office in New Delhi and met my friend Abraham.

He asked, "Pastor, how is the construction work of the children's home coming along?"

"Tomorrow we are planning to lay the foundation of the children home at Dhulawat Village," I said.

"Have you taken the C.L.U.?" he asked.

"Sorry, Brother, what is this C.L.U.?" I asked.

"Oh Pastor, you are a son of a farmer and that too of Haryana. You should have known this," he said.

"Brother, sorry to say that I have no idea about it. Yes, I had asked the tehsildar (revenue officer) at his office if we are required any permission to be taken to build. He said that our land is outside the town area. So we could start our work. So Brother, tell me, what is this C.L.U.?"

He said, "C.L.U. means 'Change of Land Use,' meaning you have to convert your farming land into a residential plot. Only then can you construct a children home there."

Then we both went to the office of the Land Planning Department at Gurgaon and inquired about the procedure of Change of Land Use.

Prayerfully we waited for the NOC (No Objection Certificate) from the government. In January 2006, the government announced through the newspaper *Dainik Jagran* that acquisitions were being made to construct an expressway road around the Delhi capitol region. Our land was in the middle of the expressway plan. The government sent us a notice and summoned us to the tehsildar tax office to receive compensation for our land. Then the government acquired the land.

With the compensation money, we bought a four acre plot in March 2008 at Sangatpura Village, Amritsar, Punjab. A Bible school and a Children's Home is in operation there today. In the coming days, we want to start a school for children. Currently, we take care of 35 children in the children's home and are providing education in an English school. We teach them the Word of God, providing a total education, meeting the spiritual, physical, and social needs of a child. These children come from various regions of Chhattisgarh, Assam, Uttar Pradesh, and Punjab.

Our vision is to provide these children with the best possible education. This is also their right. They may achieve success in the future and some may also work for the extension of His Kingdom as anointed servants of the Lord. Some of these children have single parents; others have lost both parents. Now the responsibility for these children is upon Living Hope Ministries.

Mercy Children's Home, Amritsar

Aanchal

A very sweet girl, Aanchal was three years old when her father brought her to Our Mercy Children's Home in Amritsar in August 2009. Her father described how his wife, after seeing her sick mother, was returning home by bus with Aanchal and her elder Bro. Gaurav. When the bus stopped at Fatehgarh Churian, her mother first de-boarded her Bro. Gaurav and then Aanchal. When she was about to get down with one foot on the road and other on the bus steps, the driver drove ahead. Aanchal's mother lost her balance, fell down, and came under the rear two wheels of the bus. Aanchal's mother died on the spot, and unfortunately, Aanchal saw her mother die in such a painful manner. It was beyond her understanding as a mere two year old. After a year, her father brought her to us because he was a poor labourer and was in and out of work. It was very difficult for him to feed both the children. Someone told him about us, and he arrived with Aanchal. It took Aanchal three years to overcome her mother's death after we took her in.

Pastors with Rev. Subodh John

Children from Assam

Then one day in Janary 2012, her father was flying a kite from the roof of the house, lost his balance, fell from the roof, and died. Aanchal is now an orphan. She is loved and cared for by Living Hope Ministries. There are other children like Aanchal. They are all gifts from the Lord. All the children are very happy and healthy. It is a family. Please pray for these children and, with an open heart bless them in any way the Lord leads.

14

Pastors Serving L.H.M

The Living Hope Bible School session is from July to March, during which ten to fifteen young men come to learn the Word of God every year.

We have fifteen brothers serving with us from different states of North India. Very briefly I would like to share about them. Among the brothers serving in Punjab, our first fruit was Pastor Hira Masih. We held a crusade in Gurdaspur, Punjab, in 1995. We had invited Bro. Rangeela from the Gumtala colony of Amritsar to lead the worship service. Bro. Hira Masih also came with him, and I met him during the crusade.

He shared with me his testimony of how he came to the Lord Jesus Christ. He said, "I was an illiterate. I had a rickshaw for earning a living. One day a preacher came to me and gave me a Gospel tract. The preacher said, 'You must read this.' I threw that tract in front of him and replied, 'I don't know how to read, so this tract is of no use to me.' He picked up that tract and gave it back to me and very humbly said, 'Brother, ask somebody to read it for you.'

"'I don't have time to get it read by somebody. Who will read it for me?' And again I threw it back. Again he picked up the tract and said, 'Every Sunday we read from the Bible about the Lord Jesus and spend time in worship. You come to our church on a Sunday and hear about the Lord Jesus Christ and know about Him.' He told me how to reach his church.

"This conversation caused anxiousness within me. After some time, I went to his church one Sunday. The very first day I felt very happy. The next Sunday also I went to the church and in the same manner continued for the whole month. One fine Sunday, I accepted the Lord Jesus as Lord and Saviour. The anointing of the Lord started to work within me in a wonderful manner. I continually attended the church having fellowship and serving.

"My pastor came up with a suitable proposal of a girl for me and he bore all responsibility of arrangement for my marriage. My wife, Lakhvinder Kaur, had passed ninth class, and she taught me to read and write. I started to read my Bible. When I studied the Word, it was a blessing.

"Pastor Ji, now I want to serve with you. I have heard about you by many servants of the Lord," he said.

After this meeting, we started our Bible school in the city of Amritsar and Bro. Hira Masih was one of the students. Ever since then he is serving the Lord. He set up small believer assemblies in many villages. The Lord also used him through signs and wonders. Today he is a respectable member of the Christian community. The Lord is blessing the church in which he ministers. More than three hundred young men and some young women have completed House Bible Study Course. Other brethren also serve in Punjab as well as in Assam, Chhattisgarh, in Central India, and in several places in Uttar Pradesh. The life of one pastor in particular has been full of difficulties due to the sudden death of his wife and the responsibility of raising three children under social pressures.

> *How beautiful on the mountains are the feet of the messenger who brings good news, the good news of peace and salvation, the news that the God of Israel reigns!* (Isaiah 52:7)

Pastors Serving L.H.M.

Living Hope School—Gurugram

Beware that you don't look down on any of these little ones. For I tell you that in heaven their angels are always in the presence of my heavenly Father (Matthew 18:10)

In the year 2002, the Lord led us to start a school for slum and street children. We made a survey in Gurugram, Dhanwapur Railway line to Surat Vihar and found that a large portion of the population is slum dwellers. Many children who were not going to school picked up garbage, scraps, and worked as domestic helpers. Many of these children roamed all day long and were involved in bad activities. The fathers of most of these children were either labourers or rickshaw pullers. The mothers usually worked in factories or as domestic helpers in homes where they cleaned, washed, or cooked. Therefore, these children were not cared for.

That year, we started a school with twenty-seven such children, providing them free education. We gave them books, uniforms, pencil, erasers, and meals. In the beginning, it was very difficult to control these children because they were stubborn and unruly. We knew that, if we wanted to see any change in them, we needed to have patience. Daily, prayerfully we taught them. Soon the Lord answered our prayers.

Today after fourteen years, we are successfully running the school. Currently we have 135 students and six teachers. From nursery to fourth class, we teach the children English as one of the subjects. We also teach from the Word of God. We provide refreshments daily. Now their parents are open to hear the Gospel. Students from our school are mostly admitted to one class higher when they migrate to another school, particularly government schools and others as well. It is a testimony of God's goodness and grace. Our objective is that the lives of these children may change and, through them, their families come to know the Lord Jesus.

Where there is no vision, the people perish; but he that keepeth the law, happy is he (Proverbs 29:18 KJV).

Miracle After Miracle in Gurugram

In April 2010, on a Sunday afternoon, I received a call from our Bro. Bilchus, "Pastor Ji, this evening there is a prayer meeting at our house. Please come to share the Word."

"Brother, you have not told me about this before," I said. "Today is Sunday and our driver is on leave. My driver's license was not renewed, and I cannot not drive a vehicle without a driving license. Being a servant of God, it is my duty to follow the laws of the country. This is what the Bible teaches us."

"You come by a rickshaw," he said. But the distance was too much and the way was very rough. No rickshaw would access the railway line. Finally I decided to go. I traveled the 18 kilometres and reached there though the way was rough. Bilchus lived in a small room. His belongings and cooking utensils were kept in that 10x10 foot room. Only two families gathered for prayer. We started the prayer meeting at the scheduled time. After praise and worship, I started sharing the Gospel.

More people came later, including Bilchus' friend and his wife. He was not able to walk properly so his wife helped him to sit on an empty chair. All others sat on the floor. I continued with the message as they arrived. After some time, that gentleman stood up with great difficulty and lay down on Bilchus' bed. I realised that he was not feeling well. Two girls heard the Word of the Lord and accepted Him as their personal Saviour. Praise the Lord! After the prayer meeting was over, Bilchus introduced me to his friend and urged, "Pastor Ji, please pray for this Bro. Akash." When I asked him about his sickness, his wife said that there was a wound on his leg that had gotten worse.

I asked him to show me his leg. It was in a cast and pus oozed out. He said that, because of this sickness, he had lost his job. His children were unable to go to school, and his wife had to do cleaning and washing work in houses.

"How long have you had this problem?" I asked.

"Since the last six months," he answered.

"Do you believe in the Lord Jesus?" I asked.

"Yes! I do," he said. "On the basis of your faith, I will pray that the Lord Jesus may heal you completely."

I asked Bro. Bilchus to bring me a scissors. I told Bro. Akash that I would now cut off his cast. He resisted, saying that the doctor had strictly advised against it.

"If you believe in Jesus then we have to exercise faith as it is written in the Holy Bible that without works faith is dead. There was a man who was sitting by the gate of the temple, and when Peter and John prayed in the name of the Lord Jesus, the man lame from birth was healed. Peter held the man's hand and strength came to his feet. Not only was he healed, but was leaping and jumping and praising God." (See Acts 3:7-10.)

As I ripped opened his cast and saw his leg, I felt as if I got an electric shock. His leg was in a state of rotting. I asked Bro. Bilchus to get some oil. He handed over a small bottle of mustard oil. I first applied the oil to his leg and prayed to the Lord

Jesus for healing. Then I returned home. On Monday, we received no news, but on Tuesday morning Bro. Bilchus called and excitedly announced that the brother was completely healed.

> *O Lord my God, I cried to you for help, and you restored my health* (Psalm 30:2).

The news of the healing went to his company. The manager went to find the truth whether he was healed or if it was a rumour. He got his job back and the company also gave him his six months' salary.

On Wednesday morning Bro. Bilchus called me, "Pastor, please come. Bro. Akash got his job back and wants you to pray as he is ready to go to work." I went to meet Bro. Akash. On seeing his foot, tears rolled from my eyes. He was completely healed! We praised and thanked the Lord Jesus for a miracle. Hallelujah!

> *Let them offer sacrifices of thanksgiving and sing joyfully about his glorious acts* (Psalms 107:22).

Firstborn Belongs to the Lord

After marrying Sona, we shifted our housing to government quarters in Karol Bagh, New Delhi. It was Bro. Walter Shakur's quarter, and he was a member of the Baptist church there. The flat had three rooms, out of which he rented to us one room and the veranda.

We both prayed that we would dedicate our first child to God. Hannah's life in the Bible inspired us that our firstborn would belong to God.

Pastors Serving L.H.M.

Consecrate to me all the firstborn, whatever opens the womb among the children of Israel, both of man and beast; it is mine (Exodus 13:2).

"...Reuben, Jacob's firstborn" (Genesis 35:23). Joseph called the name of the firstborn Manasseh: "For God has made me forget all my toil and my entire father's house" (Genesis 41:51). Thus says the Lord: "Israel is my son, my firstborn" (Exodus 4:22). That firstborn belonged to the Lord. With this thought we prayed to the Lord that He would give us a son.

During this time in October 1966, I went alone to Dehradun to attend the annual convention of Dehradun Masihi Mandali (first Pentecostal Christian Church). There I met Senior Pastor Rev. Wilfred Paul.

He asked me, "Where do you live?"

"In New Delhi," I answered. I introduced myself and shared with him my life's testimony.

He was glad to meet me and said, "It's good that you stay in New Delhi. I am coming soon, and I will visit you." The Lord blessed me during the convention.

After I returned to New Delhi, nearly a week later, Pastor Wilfred Paul visited us. The same evening, he had to leave for Ahmadabad, Gujarat. We spent some good time of fellowship with him. In the evening when he was leaving for the railway station, he asked us, "Please call your children and we will pray."

We were surprised because we had only been married since April. We kept looking at each other.

He again insisted, "Come on! Call out your kids."

"Pastor Ji, we just got married in April," I said.

"Okay! No problem. Get on your knees; come we will pray."

He laid his one hand on my head and the other one on my wife's and prayed for the blessing of a child for us.

The time for his train had come. The railway station was

near our residence so I went along with him. In those days, my wife taught in the Sunrise School of Mr. and Mrs. Sohan Lal in the Christian colony in New Delhi. I was serving as an evangelist with the Bible Society of India.

After some time, we discovered that Sona was pregnant. We prayed to the Lord for a son. The Lord blessed us with our first born on August 5, 1967. We dedicated our firstborn to the Lord and named him Subodh John. Praise the Lord!

In 1982, Subodh accepted the Lord in Shimla, Himachal Pradesh, during a meeting organised by Bro. Manohar from Karnataka. He experienced the anointing of the Holy Spirit. In April 1983, he obeyed the Lord in immersion baptism while we lived in Chandigarh. He completed his B.A. English with honours from Punjab University in 1987 and started working at the Park Hotel, Parliament Street, in New Delhi.

In February 1989, Dr. John Gillman came to our house with his friend Dr. Joe Umidi. We arranged a home group meeting. During the conversation, Dr. Joe asked Subodh what he was doing.

Subodh replied that he was working at the Park Hotel.

"What are your future plans?" asked Dr. Gillman.

"I want to study biblical counselling because I feel that I should be a Christian counsellor," answered Subodh.

"Okay! We shall see what we can do for you," said Dr. Gillman.

Dr. Joe Umidi, professor at CBN University in Virginia Beach, USA, helped Subodh to get admission into the Biblical Counselling course at CBN University. He needed a flight ticket to travel to the USA, and we did not have enough money. While Subodh worked at Park Hotel for two years, he always gave his salary to his mother. When the time had come for him to travel to the USA, he said to me, "Father, we have to purchase the ticket. How will we arrange for it?"

Pastors Serving L.H.M.

"I have the money," said Sona. "Subodh gave his salary to me after paying his tithe. I have kept it safe." And so, the ticket to travel for Subodh was arranged.

In September 1990, Subodh went to the USA and didn't come back for a full fourteen years. All these years we prayed for his return, but he didn't come back. We were disappointed and had lost all hope. Our firstborn, whom we dedicated for the Lord's service, had very clearly said to us that when the Lord calls me, only then would he go back to India. Some other person would need to help us in the ministry.

In 1998, CBN's medical team of Operation Blessing was serving in different countries. Subodh assisted their doctors in the operating theatre. The Operation Blessing team came to Hyderabad. During that time the Lord spoke to him, "I have chosen you for India."

On completion of the work, his team went to Indonesia, but Subodh took leave and came to visit us in Delhi. Those days we were running a Bible school in Gurgaon. He came to us only for four hours and said, "Father, I am coming back soon." We thought that he was just comforting us. Since he had come to us after eight years and for four hours only, we did not pay much attention to it.

In those days, Bro. Ashok Sharma from Jaipur and Bro. Samuel Masih from Ajmer, who was a son of a teacher, were both helping me in the ministry. Samuel was capable of doing anything. He led the worship and was a skilled tailor too. He also ran adult education classes near the Bijwasan Railway Station in the slum area. He was a very talented servant of God. Even today when I remember him I thank the Lord for his life.

Subodh called us in March 2001 and said that he was coming back. This time, he came alone. He went to Punjab and worked with the pastors there in the months of May and June.

We wondered why he came in the summer of June in such hot weather. First he came alone and the second year he came with his friend. And whenever he came, he said, "Father, I am coming back soon." Finally, in March 2004 he came with all his baggage. We were really surprised.

Subodh got married on November 8, 2004 to Sakshi Luther, who is a daughter of the late Bro. Eric Luther of Dehradun Masihi Mandali. Bro. Eric Luther was serving in Doon Bible College, Dehradun. The Lord has blessed Subodh and his wife with a daughter and a son. After that for the next eight years he supported me in the ministry. For four years, I was in Punjab, looking after the construction building of Mercy Children's Home. There on December 15, 2010 I had a heart attack and was brought to Delhi for bypass surgery. It was done on February 14, 2011. Subodh and Sudhir took care of me completely, and friends helped with medical expenses.

After recovering, I spoke to the chairman of the board of Living Hope Ministries, Dr. Enoch Anthony, and expressed my desire to hand the work over to capable hands. He approved of my suggestion and we started to pray. We also put an advertisement in Christian magazines for the need of a committed leader. Three applications were received from the outside and one of them was Subodh himself. The first applicant had some demands and also asked what the salary package would be. Our chairman answered him that there was no package because it is a faith ministry and we do not guarantee payment. We believe that the Lord is faithful to meet our needs, but we cannot promise anything. At this he took his application back.

The second applicant said that his parents would also stay with him. We answered, "We have no problem whatsoever, but you will have to travel to Chhattisgarh, Uttar Pradesh, Punjab, Assam, and various parts of northwest India. We have a children's home in Punjab; there are 35 children at present. We will not take more than 50 children."

"Let me check back with my parents and then I will confirm with you," he replied. Till today we have not heard from him.

Now Subodh was the last candidate. He was also called for an interview. He was told about the vision and all the responsibilities of the ministry.

He said, "The Lord has sent me from America to India for this after fourteen years." He told his story in full detail. He said, "I had told my father very clearly that I will never return. I have now returned on hearing the voice of the Lord and want to be a part of this ministry; and whatever responsibilities will be given, I will bear."

So on March 25, 2012, the board members of the Living Hope Ministries installed Bro. Subodh John as Executive Director, and he took charge on April 1, 2012 as the Executive Director of Living Hope Ministries.

In 2012, because of Subodh's travel with his family to Amritsar, Punjab, the education of both children were adversely affected. Subodh's daughter Kathyrn suffered a time lag of two years. But in every circumstance, our God is faithful. As the Bible says, be thankful in every situation. We praise His holy name!

Rev. Subodh John family

From Roadside to the Royal Family

Basant Lama

Basant Lama came to us in 1992. Only 17 years old, he was from a Tibetan Buddhist family of Bengal. His parents had thrown him out because he had accepted Jesus as his personal Lord and Saviour. A pastor met him and took him to Doon Bible College, Dehradoon. There Pastor T.J. Simon, one of the teachers at the Bible college, suggested that the pastor who brought Basant Lama should take him to D.C. Kaushal in Delhi.

We welcomed him. He stayed with our children and began to grow in the Lord and in his gifts. Basant's early education was incomplete. We encouraged him to take schooling through the Open School System of Education, and he completed the twelfth grade. Basant became a very committed worship leader. When we started our first Bible school in Punjab, we gave him the opportunity to join the Bible Course. Gradually we gave small responsibilities to him.

When we began our ministry among the Nepali and North-East people in Gurgaon, Basant ministered among them. According to his calling and talent, he became a worship leader and preacher of the Word. He shepherded the people, loving to care for the sheep. In 2002, under the guidance of the Lord, he returned to his home town in Bengal. Ever since, he has been ministering there among the tea garden workers and has establish a home church. He is married and they have a son.

But as for me and my family, we will serve the Lord (Joshua 24:15).

Pastors Serving L.H.M.

GREAT IS THY FAITHFULNESS

Great is thy faithfulness O God, My Father
There is no shadow of turning with Thee.
Thou changest not, Thy compassions, they fail not,
As Thou hast been Thou forever wilt be.

Great is Thy faithfulness,
Great is Thy faithfulness,
Morning by Morning new mercies I see,
All I have needed Thy hand hath provided,
Great is Thy faithfulness Lord unto me.

Summer and winter
Spring time and harvest,
Sun, moon and stars in their courses above,
Join with all nature in manifold witness,
To Thy great faithfulness, mercy and love.

Pardon for sin and a peace that endureth,
Thine own dear Presence to cheer and to guide,
Strength for today and
Bright hope for tomorrow,
Blessings all mine with ten thousand beside.

Many Thanks

To all the Lord's chosen servants, teachers, friends, colleagues, leaders, donors, and prayer partners, I would like to express gratitude from the bottom of my heart. Thank you to those who encouraged me under various circumstances, taught the Word of God, and explained the importance of prayer. I appreciate your contribution in molding my life.

I give thanks to God for everything, especially for my pastor. These are the people who loved me, and wanted my well-being. In Romans 13:7, the Bible says: "Render therefore to all their due...honor to all friends here and there."

D.C. & Sona Kaushal's family

About the Author

D.C. Kaushal was born in a Hindu family at Rohtak district of Punjab (India). Since his childhood there were many questions concerning God that use to arise in his mind, and in his quest to find those answers he received Lord Jesus Christ as his personal Savior on the roadside. He thereafter decided to commit his life to the service of this great and living God. For a long period he served Lord as Director of India Every Home Crusade, at Jaipur and Chandigarh.

He has received various degrees: a B.A. from Nagpur University, Maharashtra and a B.D from Union Biblical Seminary, Yavatmal, Maharashtra, India. He has also received M.Th and a D.Min from Western Theological Seminary, in Norris City, Illinois.

He is the founder of Living Hope Ministries, and through this ministry, along with his wife, Sona, and children, he is presently serving God through Mercy Children's Home, Slum School, Bible School, and Church planting by being faithful to God's calling. He is known for his dauntless lifestyle in India as well as around the world.

www.ingramcontent.com/pod-product-compliance
Lightning Source LLC
Chambersburg PA
CBHW050556300426
44112CB00013B/1938